CYBER CRIME

Defeat Cybercrime with Awareness

By

KRRIZTIANN V S

Table of Contents

Introduction to Cyber Crime

The first recorded law-breaking came about within the year 1820! That's not stunning considering the very fact that the abacus, that is assumed to be the earliest sort of a laptop, has been around since 3500 B.C. in India, Japan, and China.

This device allowed the repetition of a series of steps within the weaving of special materials. This resulted in a concern amongst Jacquard's workers that their ancient employment and support were being vulnerable. Today computers have come back an extended method, with neural networks and nano-computing promising to show each atom during a glass of water into a laptop capable of activity a Billion operations per second. Law-breaking is Associate in nursing evil having its origin within the growing dependence on computers in trendy life.

$10 million was fraudulently transferred out of the bank and into a checking account in Schweiz. A Russian hacker cluster light-emitting diode by Vladimir Kevin, an illustrious hacker, perpetrated the attack. The cluster compromised the bank's security systems. Vladimir was allegedly exploitation his workplace laptop at AO Saturn, a laptop firm in St. Petersburg, Russia, to interrupt into Citibank computers. He was finally inactive on Heathrow landing field on his thanks to Schweiz.

Defining Cyber Crime

At the onset, allow us to satisfactorily outline "cybercrime" and differentiate it from "conventional Crime".

The act would be unsuitable because the Indian legal code conjointly covers several cybercrimes, like email spoofing and cyber defamation, causing threatening emails etc. an easy nonetheless durable definition of law-breaking would be "unlawful acts whereby the pc is either a tool or a target or both".

Let me examine the acts whereby the pc could be a tool for associate in the nursing unlawful act. This type of activity sometimes involves a modification of a standard crime by exploitation computers.

In this book providing information about "CYBERCRIME" and its classifications and disputes. The modern era is a cyberworld. The modern providing modern technologies rapidly.You know, how cyber is working. Day by day technologies are improving it's also improving crimes in internet. "Every 3 seconds an identity is stolen". You must know about the "CYBERworld" - basic or advanced knowledge.

"Have a good read"

Cybercrime

Cybercrime isn't associate a previous variety of crime to the planet. It's outlined as any criminal activity that takes place on or over the medium of computers or web or different technology recognized by the data technology Act. Cybercrime is that the rifest crime taking part in a devastating role in the fashionable Asian nation. Not solely the criminals are inflicting huge losses to the society and therefore the government. However also are able to conceal their identity to an excellent extent. There are a variety of contraband activities that are committed over the web by technically skillful criminals. Taking a wider interpretation it may be afore said that, Cybercrime includes any criminal activity wherever laptop or web is either a tool or target or each.

The term cybercrime is also judicially taken in some judgments gone along courts in the Asian nation, but it's not outlined in any act or statute gone along the Indian legislative assembly. Cybercrime is associated controllable evil having its base within the misuse of growing dependence on computers in fashionable life. Usage of laptop associated different allied technology in existence is growing speedily and has become an urge that facilitates user convenience. It's a medium that is infinite and immeasurable. Any the great we will to the U.S.A., it's its dark sides too. A number of the newly emerged cybercrimes are cyber-stalking, terrorism, e-mail spoofing, e-mail bombing, cyber erotica, cyber- defamation etc. Some standard crimes might also return underneath the class of cybercrimes if they're committed through the medium of laptop or web.

Definition of Cyber Crime

The Oxford wordbook outlined the term cybercrime as "Criminal activities administered by means that of computers or the net."

"Cybercrime is also aforesaid to be those species, of which, the genus is that the typical crime, associate degreed wherever either the pc is an object or subject of the conduct constituting crime"

"Cybercrime means that any criminal or alternative offense that's expedited by or involves the employment of electronic communications or data systems, together with any device or the net or anyone additional of them"

History and Evolution of law-breaking

During the amount of 1950's, it might be associate stunned feeling for everybody World Health Organization uses palmtops and microchips these days, to understand that the primary the successful laptop was engineered and therefore the size of the pc was thus massive that it takes the house entire area and that they were too high-priced to work. The functioning of that laptop was unintelligible to sizable amount individuals of individuals and solely choose people expertly had direct access to such computers and has the data to work them. For obvious reasons, the pc technology was very high-priced and on the far side the buying capability of virtually the whole population till IBM's came into being whereby it introduced its complete "personal computer" in 1981 and exposing several to the rewards of fast knowledge access and manipulation that, up to it time, had been completed by few. The nation-public computers become cheaper and become manage item at the beginning of the twenty-first century in the Asian nation. The web was 1st started by the U.S.A. department of defense, once war II with the concept to possess a network that may add to the event of disaster or war and firmly transmit info. The primary Network was referred to as ARPANET, with the event of Transmission management Protocol/Internet Protocol, World Wide net and machine-readable text the web become rage everywhere on the planet. With the expansion of the web, the standard and kind of info grew. But at that time no one anticipated the opportunities' the web goes to supply the technology savvy criminals.

In the Asian nation, the web services started by the state-owned Videsh Sanchar Nigam restricted in the year 1995 and in 1998 the Gov. has all over the monopoly of VSNL and market is opened to personal operators. At that time, the web users in Asian nation are zero.1% of total population, and the currently Asian nation has become the second largest country in terms of web users once china with 33.22% individual victimization web.

The process of criminalization of human behavior judged to be harmful to the public is usually one that builds slowly in common law jurisdictions. The momentum gained through drawback identification and pressures exerted mg interest group teams will simply span decades before undesirable actions square measure classified as "crime". In some instances, this method is accelerated through the incidence of sure "catalyst events" that capture the attention of the general public and therefore the attention of lawmakers.

The first recorded cyber crime occurred within the year 1820. That's not stunning considering the very fact that the abacus, that is believed to be the earliest type of a pc, has been around since 3500 B.C. in India, Japan, and China. This device allowed the repetition of a series of steps within the weaving of special materials. This resulted in a concern amongst Jacquard's workers that their ancient employment and living were being vulnerable. This can be the primarily recorded cybercrime.

In the case of pc crime, legislators grew additional attentive is that the Nineteen Eighties as businesses became more dependent upon automation and as catalyst event cases exposed vital vulnerabilities to criminal violations. Criminals will currently simply cipher data representing proof of their criminal acts, store the knowledge and even transmit it with very little concern of detection by enforcement. Thanks to the extraordinary impact of the web, a pc crime scene will currently span from the point of the victimization (e.g., the victim's personal computer) to the other purpose on the planet, additional complicating criminal inquiring efforts. In effect, pc technology has dramatically altered the criminal justice parcel of land such enterprising and opportunist criminals have consciously turned to the pc to commit their criminal acts in things during which the computer is the instrument of the crime, the means that by that the crime is committed, moreover as in cases during which the victim's pc, or ADP system, is the target, or objective, of the act. And, as declared on top of, the presence of latest engineering aids cybercriminals in things during which the pc the pc's role is related the crime; things during which the computer is employed to deal with and shield data that's proof attachment the bad person to criminal acts. A commonality among these varieties of crimes is that the bad person, to a good degree, depends upon the shortage of technical skills of enforcement to with success commit the offenses and escape unobserved. Based mostly upon what empirical proof has been offered on self-assessed skills of investigators during this space, pc criminals would have smart reason to feel some confidence in their possibilities to evade detection of their crimes.

As we have a tendency to advance towards the twenty-first century, it can be discovered that the technological innovations have ordered the manner for the complete population exploitation engineering nowadays, to expertise new and marvelous conveniences in their way of life starting from the way to educated, shop, entertain, to availing the understanding of the business methods and workflow. Our day-to-day lives are forever modified because of speedy advances created within the field of engineering. These changes enable the United States of America to speak over nice distances in an associate instant and allow the United States of America, virtually effortlessly, to gather and organize giant amounts of knowledge, tasks that would, otherwise, prove unwieldy and costly. The technological treasures that have improved the standard of our lives, however, will moderately be viewed as a double-edged weapon system. Whereas technology has opened doors to increased conveniences for several, this same technology has conjointly opened new doors for criminals.

Nature and Scope of Cyber Crime

Crime could be a socially correlative development. In spite of what proportion we have a tendency to attempt, we have a tendency to can, not expertise a society while not law-breaking. In actual sense, once we don't seem to be nevertheless ready to manage the rate to the fascinating minimum within the universe, however, wouldn't it be done to curb a similar within the virtual world, because the same is relatively additional unreal, everlasting and de jure less-manageable. But with the time, nature and scope and definition of crime changes during a given society. Crimeless society could be a story and crime cannot be white from a society. So the character of the crime depends upon the character of a society.

The complexity of the society determines the quality of the crime that evolves' around it. To grasp the crime during a society, it's essential and crucial to verify all the factors that influence and contribute to the crime. The socio-economic and political structure of the society has to understand the crime and therefore the resource that will curb a similar. The preventive and corrective measures adopted by the machinery to regulate the crime and delinquent behavior within the society are taken into thought whereas finding out the character and scope of against the law.

The advancement of the technology has created new socio-economic and political downside within the society and rather than serving to the state in dominant the matter it's created a new advanced state of affairs that is troublesome to understand and even additional troublesome to apply current law to face the situation. The state machinery is not equipped with enough sources and information to handle the trendy crime.

Computers have reworked the trendy society on the far side expectations in last 3 to four decades. it created life not solely convenient however has additionally vastly helped completely different sections of the globe come back nearer socially, economically and culturally. The pc technology has created it doable to possess access to any or all corners of the globe whereas sitting during space. Fashionable technology has to place associate degree finish to the barriers of your time and house. However, unlikely with the exceptional deserves of getting computers nowadays, because of this the territorial issue has been created in the system.

Jurisdiction is one facet that is incredibly troublesome to work out in international dealings over the net. There was unmanageable ambiguity once courts we have a tendency tore subjected to queries relating jurisdiction law and were unable to come to a decision the right forum to entertain cases involving cybercrime because the Net or virtual world is borderless if we compare it with physical world which is why it terribly troublesome to regulate law-breaking. Through the native machinery, we have a tendency to don't seem to be ready to tackle the matter connected with cybercrime as a result of our machinery incompatible to traumatize international crimes. The law applicable to the territory is not advanced enough to control the cybercrime as their nature is way completely different from the present crime.

Thus, the world dimension of cybercrime is created it troublesome to handle and handled. The evolution of new technology has given North American country such a lot of blessings to traumatize future issues and grow with speedy rate however additionally it's provided the scope for criminals to commit their crime with least likelihood of detection. The Net has tried a boon to the deviant behavior within the society. The idea of cybercrime has gained speed and that we face the nice threat of its impact on world society. The human society is become at risk of cybercrime because of additional and additional dependence on technology.

Cybercrime becomes a world development and thus the nationwide generalization of crime cannot executable in a gift situation. Our understanding and regulation of cybercrime can't be national however must be international. The tendency to have to enact new laws and prepare preventive and defensive mechanism globally, solely then we will able to shield our society from this evil known as 'Cyber Crime'.

Therefore, the threat of cyber coercion throws a serious challenge to the world and its agencies. The terrorist organization's exploitation technology to unfold hate among folks and exploitation it to recruit militants and train them exploitation teaching tools. They're additionally launching websites that show them the way to use weapons build bombs etc.

Reasons for Cyber Crime

Hart in his work the conception of law has same —human beings area unit vulnerable therefore the rule of law is needed to guard them‖. The explanations for the vulnerability of computers could also be same to be:

1. **Capability to store information in relatively little space:** the pc has the unique characteristic of storing information in an exceedingly very little house. This affords to get rid of or derive info either through physical or virtual medium makes it abundant easier.

2. **Simple to access:** the matter encountered in guarding an automatic data processing system against unauthorized access is that there's each chance of breach undue to human error however because of the complicated technology. By on the QT planted malevolent program, key-loggers that may steal access codes, advanced voice recorders; tissue layer imagers etc. that may fool biometric systems and bypass firewalls is used to urge past many security systems.

3. **Complicated:** The computers work on operative systems and these operative systems successively are composed of variant codes. The human mind is fallible and it's impractical that there may not be a lapse at any stage. The cybercriminals profit of those lacunas and penetrate into the system.

4. **Negligence:** Negligence is incredibly closely connected with human conduct. It is therefore terribly probable that whereas protective the pc system there can be any negligence, that successively provides a cybercriminal to realize access and management over the pc system.

5. **Loss of proof:** Loss of proof may be a quite common & obvious downside as all the information are habitually destroyed. An additional assortment of information outside the territorial extent conjointly paralyzes this technique of crime investigation.

Classes of Cyber Crime

Cybercrimes are generally categorized into 3 classes, specifically crime against

1. Individual

2. Property

3. Government

Each class will use a range of strategies and also the strategies used vary from one criminal to a different.

Individual: This sort of law-breaking is within the kind of cyberstalking, distributing creation, trafficking, and grooming. Today, law social control agencies are taking this class of law-breaking terribly seriously and are change of integrity forces internationally to succeed in and arrest the perpetrators.

Property: Rather like within the world wherever a criminal will steal and rob, even within the cyber world criminals resort to stealing and robbing. during this case, they can steal a person bank details and siphon money; misuse the MasterCard to make various purchases online; run a scam to urge naïve individuals to give their hard-earned money; use a malicious software package to realize access to associate organizations website or disrupt the systems of the organization. The malicious software package may also damage software package and hardware, rather like vandals harm property within the offline world.

Government: Though not as common because the different 2 classes, crimes against a government are named as cyber-terrorist act. If fortunate, this class will bring disturbance and cause panic amongst the civilian population.

The different types of cybercrimes are:

1. **Unauthorized Access and Hacking:** Unauthorized access suggests that any kind of access while not the permission of either of the rightful or person guilty of the pc, automatic data processing system

or network. Hacking suggests that associate black-market intrusion into an automatic data processing system and/or network. Each act committed to breaking into a laptop and/or network is hacking. Hackers write or use ready- created laptop programs to attack the target laptop. They possess the will to destruct and that they get the kick out of such destruction. Some hackers hack for private financial gains, such as to stealing the credit card info, transferring cash from varied bank accounts to their own account followed by withdrawal of cash. Government websites are the foremost targeted sites for the hackers.

A hacker is associate unauthorized user UN agency attempts makes associate attempt tries to or gains access to a data system. Hacking may be a crime though there's no visible harm to the system since its associate invasion into the privacy of information. There are totally different categories of Hackers.

a) **White Hat Hackers-** They believe that info sharing is nice and that it is their duty to share their experience by facilitating access to info. However, there are some white hat hackers UN agency are simply joy riding" on laptop systems.

b) **Black Hat Hackers-** They cause harm when intrusion. They will steal or modify information or insert viruses or worms that harm the system. They're conjointly called —crackers.

c) **Gray Hat Hackers-** generally moral however often violates hacker ethics Hackers can hack into networks, complete computers, and software package. Network hackers attempt to gain unauthorized access to personal laptop networks only for the challenge, curiosity, and distribution of info. Whacky perform unauthorized intrusion with harm like stealing or ever-changing of data or inserting malware (viruses or worms).

Characteristics of Cyber Crime

The idea of cybercrime is terribly totally different from the ancient crime. Additionally, because of the expansion of Web Technology, this crime has gained serious and untied attention as compared to the normal crime. Therefore it's necessary to look at the peculiar characteristics of cybercrime.

1. **Folks with specialized data** – Cyber crimes will solely be committed through the technology, therefore to commit this sort of crime one must be terribly mean in web and computers and the web to commit such a criminal offense. That have committed cybercrime area unit well educated and have a deep understanding of the usability of the web, and that's created work of police machinery terribly troublesome to tackle the perpetrators of cybercrime.

2. **Geographical challenges** – On the Internet, the geographical boundaries reduced to zero. A cybercriminal in no time sitting in any a part of the globe commit a crime in a different corner of the world. As an example a hacker sitting in Asian country hack within the system placed in us.

3. **Virtual World** –The act of cybercrime takes place within the cyber area and therefore the criminal World Health Organization is committing this act is physically outside the cyber area. Each activity of the criminal whereas committing that crime is done over the virtual world.

4. **Assortment of proof** - it's terribly troublesome to gather proof of cybercrime and prove them in a court of law thanks to the character of cybercrime. The criminal in cybercrime invokes the jurisdiction of many countries whereas committing the cybercrime and at a similar time he's sitting someplace safe wherever he's not traceable.

5. **The magnitude of crime unimaginable -** The cyber crime has the potential of inflicting injury and loss of life to an extent that can't be fanciful. The offenses like a cyber act of terrorism, cyber smut etc has a wide reach and it will destroy the websites, steal information of the businesses in no time.

School of thought of provision in Cyber Crime

As so much as ancient Crime cares provision and activity area unit the 2 most vital parts to crime. Activity means that "Such results of human conduct because the law seeks to prevent". There should be commission or omission to represent a criminal offense. As so much as provision cares, it means that "A guilty state of mind". The mental part forms the opposite vital ingredient of crime. The act remains constant whereas the state of mind makes the act 'reus' and thus an offense. Most the crime needs proof of mental part of some kind. As so much cybercrime goes it's terribly troublesome to work out the provision in cybercrimes.

In Cyber crimes, one ought to see what the state of mind of hacker was which the hacker knew that the access was unauthorized. Thus, a "Particular Computer" wants to not be supposed by the hacker, it's enough if the unauthorized access was to "any computer". Awareness on the part of the hacker becomes easier to prove wherever he's an outsider and has no authority to access. However, wherever hacker is already has restricted authority as particle the case of the worker of a corporation, it becomes troublesome establish that he exceeded his limits and was even attentive to the actual fact that he's extraordinary it.

Actus Reus in cybercrimes has become a challenge because the entire act is committed in intangible surroundings. The culprit could leave some footmarks within the machine itself although it becomes a herculean task for the enforcement machinery to prove it within the courts because it is needed to be in physical type or at least in such a type wherever it becomes allowable obvious.

Cybercrime with Mobile and Wireless Technology

As it is evident that at the present the mobile is therefore developed that it becomes somewhat corresponding to notebook computer, as we are able to do loads of labor on our mobile phones that were earlier potential on the computers solely, like surfrider, causing e-mails etc. there's additionally increase within the services that were accessible on the mobile phones like Mobile Banking, mobile pocketbook and different economic dealing done over the phone through web that is additionally liable to cyber crimes on the mobile. Because of the event within the mobile and wireless technology day by day, the commission of cyber crimes on the mobile is changing into a serious threat at the side of different cyber crimes on the cyber web.

Varieties of Crimes committed through Mobile and Wireless

Technologies When a factor is formed or a brand new invention is completed or one thing has been explored that never earlier had been known to humans, the factor that is fabricated was for sure with the intent to produce a profit to the human race and for the expansion and prosperity of the planet. However, the history tells us that almost all of the time something fabricated, it absolutely was used for the nice cause and also the unhealthy cause that's for constructive as well as harmful functions. we are able to take a heap of example to grasp this like 'Nuclear Energy', once it absolutely was discovered it absolutely was not known to the scientists that its most large-scale use within the future won't be as another supply of energy for the good thing about human race however in creating nuclear bombs that can place question mark even on the terrible existence of humans, we are able to additionally take example of web, that was developed to facilitate the communication across the planet, however we are able to see that it's currently virtually equally for helpful activities and harmful once like frauds, creation, theft, hacking, harassment etc. this can be a similar case with Wireless Technology and also the itinerant system, that was additionally been misused loads in criminal and harmful activities.

Mobile telephones ore at the center of an apace growing rise, the purloined mobile even used as a criminal 'Currency'. At a similar time, the technical quality of a phone fraud makes detection and prosecution tough. Therefore we want the new law to traumatize the crime associated with itinerant and issues arising therefrom.

Movable thievery

The increased pressure of competition in the mobile telecom sector has junction rectifier to competitive tariffs, that successively have spurred medium growth and accumulated teledensity. The price of the French telephone perhaps the most inhibiting issue at the low finish of the market. This value has conjointly been falling steadily, there still may be a gap between the costs within the gray market (consisting of stolen/smuggled handsets) and therefore the legitimate market. So as to curtail the illegitimate gray market and defend client interest, some action is needed to be taken to discourage this crime of French telephone thievery.

Mobile phone instrument thievery is turning into a serious drawback altogether countries and maybe a key driver behind town crimes and theft. Globally this is often seen as a serious issue and therefore the drawback is being studied to search out a good answer. In the UK, a law (Mobile Phones Reprogramming Act 2002) has been created to curb the reprogramming of handsets. Reprogramming would alter re-use whereas creating it troublesome to spot any thievery of the French telephone. Alternative efforts are happening, like the institution of a worldwide Central instrumentality distinctive Register (CEIR) at the port, Ireland, and a "Mobile business Crime Action Forum" representing Operators, makers, and retailers for endeavor movable thievery and connected problems. In the European Union, information is being gathered by the United Kingdom through form responses to handle the matter of movable thievery. These varied initiatives, as well as responses to the form in EU, show that variety of cooperative efforts square measure required to tackle the matter of movable thievery. Efforts want to be taken by varied parties involved, based on the specific database, institutional structures, and cooperation among manufacturers, Network Operators, and among Government agencies. In fact, there is a necessity for even collaboration among Governments to handle this matter. Supported associate degree examination of the efforts being created internationally, it's attainable to spot a number of the most factors/agents that have emerged as being necessary for endeavor movable thievery. In summary, these include:

1. Many countries don't hold movable thievery information. Information about the relevant phones which require to be tracked is a vital ingredient of any effective effort to curb the thievery of mobile phones. A serious effort is needed to create up such information, and co-operation of all involved would be crucial for its effectiveness. In India, no authentic information is out there relating to the number of mobile handsets purloined in an exceedingly year. In those countries that have statistics on movable thievery, information is collected by the police, and therefore the scale of the matter in some cases involves up to 330,000 purloined mobile phones a year.

2. There's a world marketplace for purloined mobile phones associate degreed an acknowledgment that these phones square measure being exported. However, there's no onerous proof or intelligence on the import/export of purloined mobile phones. There are no joint operations between police forces from completely different countries thus far.

3. Reprogramming makes it troublesome to spot the first phone, as a result of through re-programming the number of the phone, i.e., the International Mobile Station instrumentality Identity (IMEI), is altered. Reprogramming is undertaken by freelance movable retailers/repair outlets and personnel people. However, again, there's no onerous intelligence on the size and nature of reprogramming activity.

4. Reprogramming activity is prohibited in an exceedingly few countries and legislation is planned or into consideration in some others.

5. There has been restricted joint operating across Ministries to tackle movable thievery thus far.

6. In most countries, discussions with the movable business in addressing the matter of mobile phones have either not taken place or have only just begun associate degreed square measure at an early stage. More actions to handle movable thievery have thus not however been in agreement.

7. In some countries, all network operators have joined the world information of purloined and lost phones while in others no network operators square measure collaborating within the Central instrumentality distinctive Register (CEIR).

8. Discussions have either not taken place or square measure just about starting. No forward actions are in agreement, however, either in terms of constructing the International Mobile Station instrumentality Identity (IMEI) tamperproof/tamper- resistant or in enhancing movable French telephone security in alternative ways in which.

The issue of movable thievery must be addressed through a united effort created globally. The additional countries take action, the larger the combined impact of this action. Countries want to work along collaboratively to tackle this shared drawback as lasting modification will solely be secured through effective multi-country co-operation, like the method initiated among European countries. Throughout the amount, once efforts square measure being created for such collaboration, we should always begin sure efforts inside our own jurisdiction and appearance for varied attainable solutions.

Use of mobile and wireless technology in Terrorist activities

Along with different crimes, one of the foremost dangerous applications of the wireless technologies and mobile phones is their use by the terrorists in acting their activities. With the assistance of those latest technologies, the terrorists were keeping in touch with their peers additional simply than within the past once communication is that the biggest barrier to the no-hit implementation of a thought. Currently, the terrorist teams around the world are well equipped with the newest technology communication gadgets like 'Satellite Phone', the communication on that is incredibly exhausting to trace. Advanced mobile technology, cooperation between international mobile communications suppliers and international money establishments and the shortage of rules create for a swift, cheap, largely untraceable cash transfer called "m-payments" anyplace, anytime, by anyone with a mobile phone. Since each terrorist act and m-payments square measure world, them-payment service supplier, as all those observance terror finances, ought to have immediate time period access to an integrated, closely monitored list of all people, organizations, businesses, and countries suspected of links to terrorists.

With the utilization of Sim cards issued on pretending addresses the terrorist will easily get in touch with their masterminds and receives directions and afterward they dispose of the Sim card and there'll be no probability for the investigation agencies to trace their location once the cardboard is destroyed. In an interrogation of a terrorist in Cashmere once a recent arrest disclose a brand new proven fact that the terrorists are currently employing an itinerant as a timer device in a very bomb, the boy tells the mechanism that they bound the itinerant to the bomb and set the itinerant on 'Vibration Mode' and therefore the bomb song to the mobile is sensitive to the frequency of the vibration of the mobile, then after they wish to detonate the bomb they accustomed to invoke the mobile tied to bomb (obviously the Sim utilized in the phone is one that earlier is issued on false identification and therefore the range of that isn't illustrious to others) then thanks to the mobile was in vibration mode so it not rings, however, vibrate, thanks to that vibration the bomb explodes. Is solely an example of on what levels the newest communication techniques can be utilized by the terrorists in their activities.

To understand that however expeditiously these latest techniques are employed by the terrorists we are able to take the instance of much-loved terrorist for the USA, Osama Usama bin Laden, he accustomed provide messages on the net, releases his audio and video tapes and offers directions to his subordinates on his satellite phone, even then one among the foremost developed country, each in economy and information technology, USA isn't able to catch him even after they tried totally and pay several bucks for this.

Re-chipping and biological research of mobile phones

Defendion options that protect the amounts are overcome and a brand new set of numbers put in. The modification of identity is termed 're-chipping' and might be achieved on analog phones in a very range of how. Sometimes, the ESN altered directly from the data input device victimization purportedly secret combos of keystrokes; in different cases, association with a laptop will enable the phone chip to be reprogrammed. The computer code to try to do this can be out there via advertisements in specialist magazines or maybe out there free over the net. Once out there, however, the instrumentation might be without delay applied to grant a purloined phone a brand new identity thus it is connected to a network, and to clone another itinerant.

A clone is an analog itinerant that has been programmed to impersonate one in hand by a legitimate subscriber by victimization its ESN and phone number (these numbers square measure typically obtained by an interception with a 'scanner' radio, felony of a dealer's or service provider's records or directly from the impersonated phone). New varieties square measure returning to the united kingdom from the USA and Hong Kong: 'tumbling' phones mechanically get an identity from a preprogrammed list, and therefore the most up-to-date 'magic' phones act as their own scanners repetition identities from close phones in use.

Mobile biological research is repetition the identity of 1 mobile phone to a different mobile phone Mobile biological research is additionally called mobile phone piracy and has been going down throughout the globe since decades. Mobile phones became a significant a part of our daily life. On the one hand, India's itinerant market has mature speedily within the last decade on the rear of falling phone tariffs and French telephone costs, creating it one among the quickest growing markets globally. On the opposite, the amount of itinerant subscribers is surpassing that of fixed-line users.

Today several mobile phones users, be it world System for Mobile communication (GSM) or Code Division Multiple Access (CDMA), run the danger of getting their phones cloned. And therefore the worst half is that it isn't abundant that you just will do to stop this. Such crime initial came to light-weight in the Republic of India in Jan, twenty05 once the city police in remission someone with 20 cell phones, a laptop, a SIM scanner, and an author. The defendant was running an exchange lawlessly wherever ii he cloned CDMA primarily based phones. He used computer code for the biological research and provided low-cost international calls to Indian immigrants in West Asia. An identical racket came to light-weight in Bombay leading to the arrest of 4 mobile dealers. Each year, the itinerant trade loses several bucks in revenue attributable to the criminal actions of persons World Health Organization square measure able to reconfigure mobile phones in order that their calls square measure beaked to different phones in hand by innocent third persons. Usually, these cloned phones square measure accustomed place many calls, usually long distance, even to foreign countries, leading to thousands of bucks in airtime and long distance charges. Cellphone firms don't need their customers to acquire any charges lawlessly created to their account, despite however nice the value. However some portion of the value of these ineligible phone calls is passed on to cellphone shoppers as a full. Several criminals use cloned cellular telephones for ineligible activities, as a result of their calls square measure not beaked to them, and square measure thus abundant tougher to trace. This development is particularly prevailing in drug crimes. Drug dealers have to be compelled to be in constant contact with their sources of the offer and their confederates on the streets. Traffickers acquire cloned phones at a minimum value, create dozens of calls, throw the phone away once as very little 'as a day' use. Within the same manner, criminals World Health Organization cause a threat to our national security, like terrorists, are illustrious to use cloned phones to thwart enforcement efforts aimed toward chasing their whereabouts.

SMS spoofing

SMS spoofing is like e-mail spoofing, that appeared to originate from your familiar with range however in point of fact it's spoofed, and send from some evil-minded individual. We are able to take this by example. Suppose if a girl receives a brief electronic communication Service (SMS) in her cell within the middle of an evening from the mobile of her relation asking her to bring money as he has met with an accident. The probabilities square measure that she would check the mobile range and if she confirms that the cell is her husband's then she would sally out with money. If this might be the response then the probabilities square measure that she isn't attentive to "Mobile Spoofing". victimization web-based computer code, a cybercriminal might send anyone a message from any person's cell while not even touching his mobile and no cellular service supplier will say that it had been spoofed or faked one.

Identity-related Crimes

A person WHO, purposely while not lawful excuse or justification or in far more than a lawful excuse or justification by employing a automatic data processing system in any stage of the offence, purposely transfers, possesses, or uses, while not lawful excuse or justification, a way of identification of another person with the intent to commit, or to assist or assist, or in reference to, any unlawful activity that constitutes against the law, commits an offence punishable, on conviction, by imprisonment for a amount not Olympian [period], or a fine not Olympian [amount], or both.

The provision covers the foremost phases of typical identity-related crimes delineated higher than. Solely the primary part, during which the bad person obtains the identity-related info, isn't coated. "Transfer" of means that of identity covers data-transmission processes from one pc to a different automatic data processing system. This act is particularly relevant to cowl the sale (and connected transfer) of identity-related info. "Possession" is the management a person purposely exercises over identity-related info. "Use" covers a large variety of practices, like submitting such info for purchase online. With respect to the mental part, the supply needs that the bad person acts purposely with respect to all objective parts and additionally has specific intent to undertake the activity to commit, aid or assist any unlawful activity that goes on the far side the transfer, possession or use of identity-related info.

Computer-related fraud

Fraud may be a common crime on the Internet. It's conjointly a standard downside on the far side the net, therefore most national laws contain provisions criminalizing fraud offenses. However, the applying of existing provisions to Internet-related cases is tough, wherever ancient national legal code provisions supported the falsity of an individual. In several cases of fraud committed over the net, it's indeed a computer system that responds to associate degree act of the wrongdoer. If ancient criminal provisions addressing fraud don't cowl laptop systems, associate degree update of the national law is critical.

Phreaking

Phreaking may be a slang term coined to explain the activity of a social group of individuals World Health Organization study, experiment with, or exploit telephones, for the needs of hobby or utility. The term 'phreak' may additionally talk to the utilization of assorted audio frequencies to govern a communication system. It's usually thought of similar, and so sorted in class with pc hacking. This is often typically referred to as the H/P culture (H for Hacking and P for Phreaking.) Most phreakers vary from the ages of 12-17. Most stop when this as a result of punishments will become additional severe once the wrongdoer isn't any longer a minor.

Many Phreaking techniques may be enforced with tiny electronic circuits, simply created by hobbyists once the key of their operation is understood. The initial circuit to generate the switch tones required to reroute long- distance calls was nicknamed the blue box by associate degree early phreak World Health Organization had engineered one in an exceedingly blue enclosure. Soon, alternative forms of Phreaking circuits got similar names. Dozens of an alternative variety of 'boxes' were unreal. fashionable Phreaking usually involves taking advantage of firms non-public Branch Exchange systems, particularly those that square measure accessible via fee numbers, to form phone calls. Phreakers don't forever do illegitimate things. In fact, they'll be thought of as a hacker within the computing world Phreakers could have an interest within the telecommunication world, concerning the additional unknown aspect of telephones.

Classification of Cyber Crime

The scientist in this chapter examines the acts whereby pc or technology is a tool for an unlawful act. The sort of activities typically involves a modification of standard crime by victimization informational technology. Here is that the list of prevailing cyber crimes, a number of them wide unfold and a few don't seem to be prevailing on a larger scale. The cyber crimes are mentioned below-

Directive on smut

The first cybercrime-related draft legal framework bestowed once the approval of the written agreement of Lisboa was the proposal for a Directive on combating the statutory offense and sexual exploitation of kids and smut that was adopted in 2011. The drafters realized that data technology allows offenders to provide and distribute smut a lot of simples and emphasizes the importance of addressing the ensuing challenges with specific provisions. It implements international standards, like the Council of Europe Convention on the Protection of kids against Sexual Exploitation and statutory offense.

Article five – Offences regarding smut

Acquisition or possession of kid creative activity shall be punishable by the most term of imprisonment of a minimum of one year. Wittingly getting access, by suggests that of knowledge and communication technology, to smut shall be punishable by the most term of imprisonment of a minimum of one year.

Offering, activity or creating obtainable smut shall be punishable by the most term of imprisonment of a minimum of two years. Production of kid creative activity shall be punishable by the most term of imprisonment of a minimum of three years.

It shall be at intervals the discretion of Member States to come to a decision whether or not this text applies to cases involving smut as stated in Article 2(c)(iii), wherever the person showing to be a baby was, in reality, eighteen years mature or older at the time of depiction.

It shall be at intervals the discretion of Member States to come to a decision whether or not paragraphs two and vi of this text apply to cases wherever it is established that sexy material as stated in Article 2(c)(iv) is made and possessed by the producer alone for his or her non-public use in thus far as no sexy material as stated in Article 2(c)(i), (ii) or (iii) has been used for the aim of its production and providing the act involves no risk of dissemination of the fabric.

Like the Convention, the Directive proposes the criminalization of getting access to smut by suggests that of knowledge and communication technology. This permits law-enforcement agencies to prosecute wrongdoers in cases wherever they're able to prove that the offender opened websites large creative activity, however, are unable to prove that the wrongdoer downloaded material. Such difficulties in aggregation proof arise, for instance, if the wrongdoer is victimization cryptography technology to safeguard downloaded files on his storage media. The informative report back to the Convention on the Protection of kids points out that the supply ought to even be applicable in cases wherever the wrong doer solely views smut footage on-line while not downloading them. In general, gap a website will mechanically initiate a transfer method – usually while not the information of the user. As a consequence, the supply is principally relevant in cases wherever consumption of kid creative activity will crop up while not transfer fabric. This can, for instance, be the case if the website allows streaming videos and, because of the technical configuration of the streaming method, doesn't buffer the received data, however, discards it straight once transmission.

Article twenty-five – Measures against websites containing or spreading smut

1. The Member States shall take the necessary measures to guarantee the prompt removal of net pages containing or spreading smut hosted in their territory and to endeavor to get the remove.

2. The Member States might take measures to dam access to sites containing or spreading smut towards the web users at intervals their territory. These measures should be set by clear procedures and supply adequate safeguards, particularly to make sure that the restriction is restricted to what's necessary and proportionate, which users are helps of the explanation for the restriction. Those safeguards shall conjointly embody the chance of judicial redress.

In addition to the criminalization of acts associated with smut, the initiation draft contained a provision that obliges the Member States to implement the method of interference websites containing smut. Many European countries, moreover as non-European countries like China, Asian nation, and Siam, use such associate approach. Issues related to the actual fact that none of the technical ideas has proved to be effective, and the approach entails a concomitant risk of over-blocking. As a consequence, the necessary interference was modified and it had been left to the Member States to come to a decision if interference obligations ought to be enforced on the national level.

Child

The term kid is very relevant with respect to the criminalization of kid creative activity. It's conjointly employed in the context of provisions that criminalize making sure content (for example adult pornography) obtainable to minors. One amongst the foremost often used definitions is provided within the UN Convention on the Rights of the kid from 1989.

For the needs of the current Convention, a baby suggests that each person below the age of eighteen years unless beneath the law applicable to the kid, the majority is earned earlier.

Several cybercrime-specific legal frameworks and model laws, like the 2011 EU Directive on combating smut, the 2007 Council of Europe Convention on the Protection of kids and also the 2009 HIPCAR Model Legislative Text on law-breaking contain similar definitions. The Council of Europe Convention on law-breaking doesn't outline kid however solely smut.

Smut

Child pornography is one amongst the few offenses associated with the class of criminal content wherever most countries within the world conform to a criminalization. Because the differentiation between legal sorts of sexual- connected material and smut may be difficult, some legal frameworks offer a definition of kid creative activity.

One major challenge for law drafters during this regard is to avoid conflicts between totally different completely different classes mature so as to avoid a probably unintended criminalization in cases wherever the age of wedding or sexual consent and also the age-limit at intervals the definition of kid creative activity differ. If, for instance, smut is outlined as visual depiction of sexual acts of an individual below the age of eighteen and at an equivalent time the age of sexual consent and the wedding is sixteen, seventeen year recent kids will de jure unite or have a relationship however are committing a heavy crime (production of kid pornography) if they take footage or movies of this act.

One definition is provided by Article two c) of the ex gratia Protocol to the Convention on the Rights of the Child on the Sale of kids, kid harlotry, and smut.

Article 2

For the aim of the current Protocol:

Smut suggests that any illustration, by no matter suggests that, of a baby engaged in real or simulated express sexual activities or any illustration of the sexual elements of a baby for primarily sexual functions.

The definition provided within the ex gratia Protocol doesn't expressly cowl sorts of fictional smut like realistic pictures. To make sure that such material is additionally lined with some legal frameworks, like the Council of Europe Convention on law-breaking, have amended the definition of kid creative activity.

Article nine – Offences associated with kiddy porn

For the aim of paragraph one higher than, the term "child pornography" shall embrace sexy material that visually depicts:

a) A minor engaged in sexually express conduct;

b) An individual showing to be a minor engaged in sexually express conduct;

c) Realistic pictures representing a minor engaged in the sexually express conduct.

For the aim of paragraph two higher than, the term "minor" shall embrace all persons underneath eighteen years aged. A celebration might, however, need a lower age-limit, that shall be not but sixteen years.

Article 9, paragraph two, provides 3 subsections on material that visually depicts kid pornography: a minor engaged in sexually express conduct, an individual showing to be a minor engaged in sexually express conduct and realistic pictures representing a minor engaged in the sexually express conduct.

While during this regard the Convention on law-breaking expands the definition provided within the elective Protocol to the UN Convention, on the opposite hand it narrows the pertinency in 2 necessary aspects.

Although the drafters of the Convention on law-breaking stressed the importance of customary identical the same a regular an even international standard concerning age the Convention on law-breaking, however, permits parties to need a distinct ordinance of not below sixteen years.

The second major distinction to the definition provided within the elective Protocol is that the proven fact that the definition within the Council of Europe Convention on law-breaking focuses on visual depiction. Kiddy porn isn't necessarily distributed as photos or movies, however conjointly as audio files. Because of the actual fact that the supply provided in Article nine refers to "material that visually depicts" a toddler, the supply doesn't cowl audio files.

As a consequence, newer approaches like the HIPCAR law-breaking legislative text follow the thought of the choice Protocol to the UN Convention rather than the Council of Europe Convention and avoid the term "visually".

Definitions

Kiddy porn means that sexy material that depicts presents or represents:

a) A toddler engaged in sexually express conduct;

b) An individual showing to be a toddler engaged in sexually express conduct; or

c) Pictures representing a toddler engaged in sexually express conduct;

This includes, however, isn't restricted to, any audio, visual or texts sexy material. A rustic might limit the criminalization by not implementing (b) and (c).

Definitions of kid erotica also are contained within the 2011 EU Directive on combating kiddy porn, and also the 2007 Council of Europe Convention on the Protection of kids.

Cyber smut

The word 'Pornography' derived from the Greek words 'Porno' and 'Graphein' suggests that writing regarding prostitutes, or said any work of art or literature managing sex and sexual themes. Shaping the term smut is incredibly troublesome and it doesn't have any specific definition within the eyes of the law as each country has their own customs and tradition. The act of smut in some countries is legal however in some it's felonious and punishable.

Cyber smut is in straightforward words outlined because the act of victimization Internet to make, display, distribute, import, or publish smut or obscene materials. With the arrival of the Internet, ancient sexy content has currently been for the most part replaced by online/digital sexy content. Smut has no legal or consistent definition.

The definition of pornography depends however on the society, norms and their values are reacting to the sexy content.

The reason why we have a tendency to do not have a clear definition as way as smut is bothered is that we have a tendency to don't have uniform normal culture and ethics within the world nor will we have uniform laws that define the smut. The construct of obscenity and smut varies from country to country and time to time. The terms obscenity and smut are totally different however associated with one another. A similar material that was illegal in some countries is also allowed in some. The Indian law doesn't outline the term smut and not handle this term.

In the present sex sells and sells extraordinarily well, and therefore the truth is that gift smut business is larger than the other company or combination of corporations within the world. The arrival of the net within the world has started the new chapter within the smut business. The smut business notice excellent place in net to unfold sexy material everywhere the planet. In line with the web filter review report of 2010, there are 4.2 million websites providing smut content to the planet. Sixty-eight million daily program requests are created and seventy-two million worldwide users visit adult sites per month. 42.7 % of total users World Health Organization use net watch sexy material over the web.

In the initial years or we are able to say before netting on the market to the general public, DVD's and Videotapes are the popular media of distributing smut. However subsequently net is on the market is out there is on the market is obtain able is accessible is offered to the general public and it becomes the foremost widespread medium to create smut available to the user within the comfort of their homes. A private world Health Organization thanks to the peer pressure or shame doesn't have access to the sexy material, these days simply watch image or video on the web. The increase of smut websites providing photos, video clips and streaming media as well as live net cam access allowed larger access of smut. Data technology has created it easier to produce and distribute sexy materials through the internet; like material are often transmitted everywhere the planet in an exceedingly matter of seconds, the geographical restrictions that prevented to a particular extent, foreign publication to enter native territories have disappeared.

Obscenity and creation

To understand the gravity and result of creation and obscenity on society, we want to grasp these terms in their widest attainable amplitude. The Word creation has not been outlined wrongfully in any a part of the globe. The essential reason behind this can be terribly simple; neither we tend to do have any uniform customary of ethical cultural, values and ethics and nor we've got any uniform customary of law.

The term obscene means that regarding materials that may be regulated or criminalized as a result of their depiction of nakedness, sex, or excretion is manifestly offensive and while not creative or scientific worth.

The take a look at of obscenity was initial set down within the case of Regina V. Hicklin because the tendency "to corrupt and corrupt those whose minds area unit receptive such influences and into whose hands a publication of this type could fall", and it absolutely was understood that this take a look at would apply solely to the isolated passage of the work.

In Miller v. California, the Supreme Court of us in landmark judgment gave the basic tips and 3 purpose tests to determine obscenity within the work i.e.

1. That the common person, applying up to date "community standards", would realize that the work, taken as a full, appeals to the lustful interest.

2. That the work depicts or describes, in the associate degree offensive method, sexual conduct or discharge functions, as specifically outlined by applicable state law or applicable law.

3. Whether or not the work, taken as a full, lacks serious literary, artistic, political, or scientific worth.

Before the miller's (supra) case, in Roth v. United States The Supreme Court of us in landmark case-control that "obscene material wasn't protected by the primary change and will be regulated by the States instead of by a singular, Federal customary and conjointly a replacement judicial customary for outlining obscenity that invoked the common person's application of up to date community standards to evaluate whether or not or not the dominant theme of the fabric taken as a full appeals to lustful interest."

The Supreme more control that "to decide obscenity derived we want to contemplate the subsequent five-part structure:

(1)The angle of analysis was that of a standard, reasonable person.

(2) Community standards of satisfactoriness were to be accustomed live obscenity.

(3) Obscenity law can solely apply to the works whose theme is in question.

(4) A work, so as to be evaluated for obscenity, had to be taken in its entireness.

(5) Associate degree obscene work was one that aimed to excited individuals' Prurient interest.

However, in Bharat miller take a look at wasn't adopted by the Supreme Court, instead, it's adopted the Hicklin's take a look at in leading case of Ranjeet D. Udeshi v. the State of Maharashtra22; the Supreme Court has set several problems concerning the obscenity. The apex court doesn't take into account obscenity an obscure construct, however, a word that is well-understood notwithstanding persons disagree in their perspective to what's obscene and what's not. The apex court has declared that "In judgment a piece, stress shouldn't be set upon a word here and a word there, or a passage here and a passage there. The work as a full should be thought of, the obscene matter should be thought of by itself and one by one to search out whether or not it's therefore gross and its obscenity, therefore, set that it's doubtless to corrupt and corrupt those whose minds area unit receptive influences of this type. During this affiliation, the interests of up to date society and significantly the influence of the impugned book on it should not be unnoticed. It's necessary that a balance ought to be maintained between "freedom of speech and expression" and "public decency or morality"; however, once the latter is considerably transgressed the previous should fall down."

The court but, plumbed a note of caution that treating with sex and nakedness in art and literature can't be thought to be proof of obscenity while not one thing additional. Within the words of the court "It isn't necessary that the angels and saints of architect ought to be created to wear breeches before they will be viewed. If the rigid take a look at of treating with sex because the minimum ingredient was accepted hardly any author of fiction nowadays would escape the fate Lawrence had in his days. [*fr1] the book-shops would shut and therefore the alternative half would deal in nothing however ethical and spiritual books."

In this case, the Supreme Court has set that Hicklin's take a look at cannot be discarded, associated aforesaid "It makes the court the choose of obscenity in regard to an impugned book etc. and lays stress on the potentiality of the impugned object to demoralize and corrupt by immoral influences. It'll invariably stay issue to make a decision onto make your mind upto choose to determine in every case associated it doesn't compel an adverse decision all told cases."

In Samresh Satyendra N. Bose v. Amal Mitra, the Supreme Court has commanded that "A vulgar writing is not essentially obscene. Inelegance arouses a feeling of disgust and repulsion and additionally tedium, however, doesn't have the result of depriving, dishonorable and corrupting the morals of any reader of the novels, whereas obscenity has the tendency to demoralize and corrupt those whose minds are hospitable such immoral influences". during this case, the court differentiated between inelegance and obscenity and additional command that whereas judgment the question of obscenity "the choose ought to ... place himself within the position of a reader of each people in whose hands the book is probably going to fall and will try and appreciate what quite attainable influence the book is probably going to possess within the minds of the readers".

In India, the Indian Penal Code, 1860 deal with the issue of obscenity. But with the evolution of new technology, obscenity and porn take electronic kind and it becomes not possible to convict the culprit beneath Indian legal code, 1860(supra). To subsume this new technology, the govt. of Republic of India has enacted data Technology Act 2000 25. Section sixty-seven of knowledge Technology Act, 2000; subsume obscenity and sexy content on the net. Section sixty-seven of the IT Act provides:

"Whoever publishes or transmits or causes to be revealed within the electronic kind, any material that is lewd or appeals to the salacious interest or if its result is like to tend to demoralize and corrupt persons World Health Organization are likely, having respect to all relevant circumstances, to read, see or hear the matter contained or embodied in it, shall be penalised on 1st conviction with imprisonment of either description for a term which can touch 2 3 years and with fine which can touch 5 large integer rupees and within the event of a second or subsequent conviction with imprisonment of either description for a term which can touch 5 years and additionally with fine which can touch 10 large integer rupees."

The Section sixty-seven of IT Act 2000 is like Section 292 of Indian legal code, 1860. In Ranjit D. Udeshi v. State of geographical area command that not like the different provision that lambast like "knowingly" or "negligently" and so build provision a condition precedent to determine the guilt. Section 292 doesn't build data of obscenity associate ingredient of the offense. The prosecution doesn't prove one thing that the law doesn't burden it with. The problem of getting legal proof of the offender's data of the obscenity of the book etc. has created the liability strict. The absence of such data is also taken in mitigation, however, doesn't take the case out of the availability. If we tend to apply the Ranjit D. Udeshi case judgment (supra) to Section 67 of IT Act, 2000, it will be terminated that mere publication associated transmission of obscene material is an offence, even so, the psychological state of the wrongdoer. However, this can not be a blanket rule applicable to any or all and varied.

Smut a menace in modern times

The children particularly adolescents are in modern times need to explore everything on data road. The youngsters in today's generation have access to net and computer's reception, the net and pc are a part of their studies. The access to pc and net makes them liable to the potential danger of net. The youngsters are someday curious about the physiological property and sexual express material. The oldsters don't have an excessive amount of management over the youngsters the kids and also the children are busy exploring the net and different medium to meet their needs through the online access. Sex–offenders exploit these conditions and fulfill the requirement of youngsters. The kid at this tender age doesn't perceive and recognize the potential danger of those contacts. The net is very utilized by the abusers to abuse youngsters sexually worldwide. The youngsters in the Republic of India become viable victim to the cybercrime, as net becomes the home item in the Republic of India. The youngsters are getting victims to the aggression of pedophiles.

In the physical world, oldsters apprehend the hazards, in order that they warn their youngsters regarding the danger and tell American state a way to avoid or face the issues by facing straightforward pointers. However, as way as cybercrime or crime associated with the net is involved the oldsters themselves doesn't apprehend regarding the issues or danger expose by varied service offered over the web. The pedophiles benefit from those things and lure youngsters and win their confidence and so exploit them as a result of oldsters or academics doesn't tell them regarding what's wrong or right over the web.

Obscenity and Freedom of Speech and Expression

Freedom of speech and expression is recognized as basic right subject to affordable restriction to keep law and order, public health morality, decency etc. in Indian Constitution. But freedom of speech and expression is restricted by section 292 and 499 of Indian legal code 1860. It implies that one can't whereas exercise their basic right of freedom of speech and expression asperse anyone and prohibits expression through obscene material or publication and distribution of obscene material.

The Fundamental right of freedom and speech isn't absolute and affordable restriction are obligatory by article 19(2) of Indian constitution that says that affordable restrictions on the exercise of the proper bestowed below article 19(1) within the interests of the sovereignty and integrity of India, the protection of the State, friendly relations with foreign States, public order, decency or morality, or in respect to contempt of court, defamation or incitement to associate degree offence.

In Maqbool Fida Husain v dominion Kumar Pandey the very fact of the case is that famed painter MF Husain painted associate degree artwork of a nude girl in grief while not giving it any title. The untitled painting was oversubscribed to a non-public collector in 2004. In 2006 it had been enclosed as a part of an internet charity auction for victims of the Kashmir earthquake below the name 'Bharat Mata.' Husain had no role or involvement during this auction. There have been large-scale protests against the painting, that appeared in an advert for the auction. There were multiple complaints filed under section 292, 294, 298 of the Indian Penal Code, 1860. The question was that whether or not a portrayal of the nude girl within the painting as "Bharat Mata" ought to be thought-about as obscene underneath section 292 of IPC. The Court command that "...the aesthetic bit to the painting dwarfs the questionable obscenity within the type of condition and renders it thus fiddling and insignificant that the condition within the painting will simply be unnoticed." The nude lady wasn't shown in any peculiar quite posture, nor was her surroundings painted thus on arouse sexual feelings or lust. The location of the Ashoka Chakra was additionally not on any specific a part of the body of the lady that would be deemed to indicate disrespect to the national emblem. The Court realized that "...the literature of, each laic and secular, is filled with sexual allusions, sexual, and passages of such frank eroticism the likes of that don't seem to be to be found elsewhere in world literature." It went on to state that "While associate creative person ought to have inventive freedom, he's not liberal to do something he needs. The road that has to be drawn is between the arts as an associate expression of beauty associated art as an associate expression of an unwell mind intoxicated with a vulgar manifestation of counter-culture wherever the latter has to be unbrokenly removed from a civilian society." The Court additionally aforesaid, "There ought to be free for the thought we tend to hate. Freedom of speech has no which means if there's no freedom when speech. The truth of democracy is to be measured by the extent of freedom and accommodation it extends."

"An act of recognition of ethical goodness by a statutory agency isn't opinion proof, however, associate instance or dealings wherever the actual fact in issue has been declared, recognized or a firmed. The Court can examine the film and choose whether or not its public policy, within the given time and environmental condition, thus breaches public morals or depraves basic decency to offending the penal provisions. Yet, particularly once a special statute (the Cinematograph Act) has set special standards for films for public consumption and created a special Board to screen and censor from the angle of public morals and also the like, with its verdicts being subject to higher review, amateurish criminal courts should take care to "rush in" and should so "fear to tread" lest the judicial method become a public path for any stickup man carrying an ethical mask holding up a film-maker United Nations agency has traveled the overpriced and dangerous journey to the exhibition of his "certificated" image. Iyer went on to state, "Art, morals, and laws, aesthetics area unit sensitive subjects wherever jurisprudence meets alternative social sciences and ne'er goes alone to bark and bite as a result of state-made strait-jacket is inhibitive prescription for a free country unless enlightened society actively participates within the administration of justice to aesthetics."

The Indecent illustration of lady Act, 1986 additionally associated with creation and obscenity as section three and four of the act has specifically prohibited the indecent illustration of a lady through publicity or in publication, writing, paintings, and figure or in the other manner and or matters connected with that or incident to it. Each web site on the web constitutes the indecent illustration of lady would fall within the range of those sections.

In Bazzee.com case, the story started once a sexually express video clip of 2 faculty students was shot with a telephone camera then distributed among friends through the multimedia system electronic communication Service (MMS). The clip, showing a lassie engaged in sexual perversion with a boy, was shot along with her consent, however, was circulated to the others while not her permission. The clip then landed within the hands of a wise bourgeois UN agency tried to form simple cash out of it. Mr. Ravi Raj, a final year M.Sc. geology student of Indian Institute of Technology, Kharagpur had opened AN account below the name 'Alice Electronics' on the auction website Bazee.com on 21'set of a Gregorian calendar month, 2004. He announces the clip therein account on the twenty-seventh of a Gregorian calendar month, 2004 below the header 'DPS lady having fun' and it remained there until twenty-ninth Gregorian calendar month, 2004. Mr. Raj was in remission on fourteenth Dec and made before a Delhi court 2 days later. The Court remanded him to 3 days police custody. Meanwhile, the business executive of Bazee.com, Mr. Avnish Bajaj, was sentenced to jail for 6 days by a Delhi court. Mr. Bajaj wanted his unharness on bail on the bottom that he had been co-operating with the police within the investigation of the case and had flown in from urban center to help the probe. He was granted bail later. The DPS boy UN agency was at the center of the MMS difference of opinion was additionally in remission and acquired before a court in Delhi. Describing the alleged act as a 'misadventure' and not 'moral deprivation', The Principal justice of Juvenile Justice Board granted him bail. On Dec 24, 2004 the opposite suspect adult male. Ravi dominion was additionally granted bail by a Delhi court considering the fact that the prime suspect has already been free on bail. The impact of the incident was that the Delhi government by its notification dated Feb 1, 2005 illegal the employment of mobile phones not solely by students however additionally by lectures altogether government-run or power-assisted faculties. the foremost ironical a part of the story is that it terminated while not even knowing what the feminine student visible within the clip had to mention or confess. Thus, Delhi Public faculty scandal wasn't solely the problem of kid porno however additionally MMS clip in a computer network.

In Feb 2008, a quick track court in Chennai Sentence orthopedic MD Dr. Prakash to immurement just in case with reference to taking an obscene image of the ladies and uploading them on to the web. Dr. Prakash became the primary person to be in remission below the data Technology Act. He was suspect of sexually exploiting ladies and uploading their obscene footage on the web with the assistance of his brother primarily based within the U.S. He was charged with offences punishable below Section sixty-seven of the data Technology Act, besides the provisions of the Indecent illustration of girls (Prohibition) Act, 1986 browse with Section twenty-seven of the Arms Act, 1959, and 120-B of the Indian legal code.

Addressing a national seminar on the social control of the cyberlaw former magistrate adult male. K.G. Balakrishnan has aforesaid that "the government may place restrictions on websites that solely circulated porno and hate speech, it'd not be right to clamp blanket bans on all classes of internet sites."

He expressed that "it was additionally necessary to tell apart between intermediaries like network service suppliers, website operators and individual users for putting liability for wrongful acts. Additional aforesaid that Liability cannot be automatically placed on web intermediaries, once it's specific people UN agency have interaction in wrongful conduct. That would be comparable to laborious the persons UN agency build roads for the rash and negligent driving of different persons UN agency operate vehicles on the roads."

The additional states that "Democratic values like freedom of speech and expression, freedom of association and therefore the freedom to pursue an occupation, business, profession or trade should be promoted within the online domain yet."

The Supreme Court of Asian nation in Kamlesh Vaswani v. Union of Asian nation & Ors. Told the Centre on twenty-seventh Feb 2016 to require steps and frame rules to prevent access to websites that includes kiddie porn, classifying them as "obscene" and a threat to social morality. A Bench of Justices Dipak Misra and S.K. Singh was reacting to a submission created by the Supreme Court ladies Lawyers Association that there have been instances wherever bus drivers and conductors forced kids below their care to observe smut and sexually mistreated them thanks to simple and free access to smut, together with kiddie porn, within the country.

Hearing this, Justice Misra aforesaid, "freedom of speech isn't absolute, liberty isn't absolute" once such rights were victimized to subject innocent kids to such sexual perversions.

The Supreme Court aforesaid, drawing the road on wherever rights terminated and criminalism began has aforesaid that "Innocent kids cannot be created prey to the present reasonably painful things and a nation cannot afford to hold on any reasonably experiment with its kids within the name of liberty,"

Further expressed that "The Centre is needed to form bound rules and laws to at first stop kiddie porn,"

The Supreme Court, however, aforesaid a transparent distinction had to be created between art and obscenity and expressed that "There unit those that feel that even Mona Lisa (painting) is porno. A distinction needs to be drawn between art and obscenity."

Spam

Having respect for the very fact that up to seventy-five percent of all e-mails area unit according to be spam e-mails, the requirement for criminal sanctions on spam e-mails has been mentioned intensively. National legislative solutions addressing spam dissent. One amongst the most reasons why spam continues to be a tangle is that filter technology still cannot establish and block all spam e-mails. Protection measures provide solely restricted protection against uninvited e-mails. In 2005, OECD printed a report that analyzed the impact of spam on developing countries. The report points out that representatives from developing countries typically specific the read that net users in their countries area unit suffering far more from the impact of spam and web abuse. An analysis of the results of the report proves that the impression of the representatives is correct. Because of a lot of restricted and costlier resources, spam seems to be a far a lot of serious issue in developing countries than in western countries.

However, it's not solely the identification of spam e-mail that poses issues. Distinctive between e-mails that area unit unwanted by recipients, however, sent lawfully, and those that area unit sent unlawfully, is a challenge. This trend towards computer-based transmission (including e-mail and VoIP) highlights the importance of protective communications from attack. If spam exceeds a definite level, spam e-mails will seriously hinder the employment of ICTs and scale back user productivity.

Identity stealing

Taking into thought media coverage, the results of recent surveys and therefore the various legal and technical publications in this field, it looks applicable to refer to identity stealing as a mass development. Despite the worldwide aspects of the development, not all countries have nevertheless enforced provisions in their national legal code system that criminalize all acts associated with fraud. The Commission of the EU Union (the EC) recently declared that fraud has not nevertheless been criminalized all told the EU Member States. The EEC expressed its read that "EU enforcement cooperation would be higher served, were fraud criminalized all told the Member States" and declared that it'll shortly begin consultations to assess whether or not such legislation is acceptable.

One of the issues with an examination of the present legal instruments in the fight against fraud is that the incontrovertible fact that they dissent dramatically. The sole consistent part of existing approaches is that the incontrovertible fact that the condemned behavior relates to 1 or a lot of the subsequent phases:

• Phase 1: Act of getting identity-related info.

• Phase 2: Act of possessing or transferring the identity-related info.

• Phase 3: Act of victimization the identity-related info for criminal functions.

Based on this observation, their area unit generally 2 systematic approaches to criminalize identity theft:

• The creation of one provision that criminalizes the act of getting, possessing and victimization identity-related info (for criminal purposes).

• The individual lawmaking of typical acts associated with getting identity-related info (like outlawed access, the assembly and dissemination of malicious code, computer-related forgery, knowledge spying and knowledge interference) in addition as acts associated with the possession and use of such info (like computer-related fraud).

Examples of single-provision approaches;

The most well-known examples of single-provision approaches area unit eighteen USC § 1028(a)(7) and 18 USC 1028A(a)(1). The provisions cowl a large vary of offenses associated with fraud. At intervals this approach, lawmaking isn't restricted to any given part, however, covers all of the 3 preceding phases. Withal, it's vital to spotlight that the supply doesn't cowl all identity-theft connected activities – particularly not those wherever the victim and not the bad person is acting.

Wittingly and while not lawful authority produces an identification document, authentication the feature, or a false identification document;

Wittingly transfers an identification document, authentication feature, or a false identification document knowing that such document or feature was taken or created while not lawful authority;

Wittingly possesses with intent to use unlawfully or transfer unlawfully 5 or a lot of identification documents (other than those issued lawfully for the employment of the possessor), authentication options, or false identification documents;

Wittingly possesses an identification document (other than one issued lawfully for the employment of the possessor), authentication feature, or a false identification document, with the intent such document or feature be wont to diddle the United States;

Wittingly possesses an identification document or authentication feature that's or seems to be an identification document or authentication feature of the us that is taken or created while not lawful authority knowing that such document or feature was taken or created while not such authority;

Any unlawful activity that constitutes a violation of Federal law, or that constitutes a crime below any applicable State or native law; or wittingly traffics in false or actual authentication options to be used in the false identification documents, document-making implements, or means that of identification;

Shall be chastised as provided in section (b) of this section.

Phase 1

In order to commit crimes associated with fraud, the bad person must get possession of identity- connected knowledge. By criminalizing the "transfer" of means that of identification with the intent to commit an offense, the provisions criminalize the acts associated with part one in an exceedingly very broad method. Because of the very fact that the provisions specialize in the transfer act, they are doing not cowl acts undertaken by the bad person before initiation of the transfer method. Acts like causation out phishing emails and planning malicious code which will be wont to get pc identity connected knowledge from the victims aren't coated by eighteen USC § 1028(a)(7) and eighteen USC 1028A(a)(1).

Phase 2

By criminalizing possession with the intent to commit an offense, the provisions once more take a broad approach with respect to the lawmaking of acts associated with the second part. This includes, especially, the possession of identity-related info with the intention to use it later in one amongst the classic offenses associated with fraud. The possession of identity-related knowledge while not the intent to use them isn't coated.

Phase 3

By criminalizing the "use" with the intent to commit an offense, the provisions cowl the acts associated with part three. Eighteen USC § 1028(a)(7) is, as mentioned higher than, not connected to a selected offense (like fraud).

Another example is section fourteen of the crime legislative text that was developed by the beneficiary states at intervals the HIPCAR initiative.

Identity-related Crimes

A person WHO, purposely while not lawful excuse or justification or in far more than a lawful excuse or justification by employing a automatic data processing system in any stage of the offence, purposely transfers, possesses, or uses, while not lawful excuse or justification, a way of identification of another person with the intent to commit, or to assist or assist, or in reference to, any unlawful activity that constitutes against the law, commits an offence punishable, on conviction, by imprisonment for a amount not Olympian [period], or a fine not Olympian [amount], or both.

The provision covers the foremost phases of typical identity-related crimes delineated higher than. Solely the primary part, during which the bad person obtains the identity-related info, isn't coated. "Transfer" of means that of identity covers data-transmission processes from one pc to a different automatic data processing system. This act is particularly relevant to cowl the sale (and connected transfer) of identity-related info. "Possession" is the management a person purposely exercises over identity-related info. "Use" covers a large variety of practices, like submitting such info for purchase online. With respect to the mental part, the supply needs that the bad person acts purposely with respect to all objective parts and additionally has specific intent to undertake the activity to commit, aid or assist any unlawful activity that goes on the far side the transfer, possession or use of identity-related info.

Encryption technology

Another issue that may complicate the investigation of law-breaking is encoding technology, that protects data from access by unauthorized folks and maybe a key technical answer within the fight against law-breaking. The encoding may be a technique of turning a visible text into Associate in nursing obscured format by victimization Associate in the Nursing rule. Like obscurity, encoding isn't new, however, engineering has remodeled the sector. For an extended time, it absolutely was subject to secrecy. In Associate in the Nursing interconnected atmosphere, such secrecy is tough to take care of.

The widespread availableness of easy-to-use software package tools and also the integration of encoding technology within the in operation systems currently makes it potential to inscribe laptop information with the press of a mouse and thereby will increase the prospect of law-enforcement agencies being confronted with the encrypted material. Various software package merchandise square measure on the market that modifies users to safeguard files against unauthorized access. But it's unsure to what extent offenders already use encoding technology to mask their activities. One survey on erotica prompt that solely six percent of in remission child-pornography possessors used encoding technology, however, consultants highlight the threat of Associate in nursing increasing use of encoding technology in law-breaking cases.

There square measure totally different technical ways to hide encrypted information and several other software package tools square measure on the market to change these processes. Ways vary from analyzing weakness within the software package tools won't to inscribe files, sorting out encoding passphrases and attempting typical passwords, too complicated and drawn-out brute-force attacks. The term "brute-force attack" is employed to explain the method of distinguishing a code by testing each potential combination. Looking at encoding technique and key size, this method may take decades. For example, if Associate in nursing bad person uses encoding software package with a 20-bit encoding, the dimensions of the keyspace is around a million. Employing a current laptop process a million operations per second, the encoding might be broken but one second. However, if offenders use a 40-bit encoding, it may take up to 2weeks to interrupt the encoding. In 2002, the Wall Street Journal was for example for instance, as Associate in nursing example able to with success decode files found on an Al al-Qaeda laptop that was encrypted with 40-bit encoding. Employing a 56-bit encoding, one laptop would take up to 2 a pair of 85 years to interrupt the encoding. If offenders use a 128-bit encoding, a billion laptop systems in operation exclusively on the encoding may take thousands of billions of years to interrupt it. The most recent version of the popular encoding software package PGP permits one 024-bit encoding.

Current encoding software package goes way on the far side the encoding of single files. The latest version of Microsoft's in operation systems, as an example, permits the encoding of a complete hard disc. Users will simply install encoding software package. Though some laptop rhetorical consultants believe that this performance doesn't threaten them, the widespread availableness of this technology for any user may lead to the larger use of encoding. Tools are on the market to inscribe communications – as an example, e-mails and phone calls – that may be sent victimization VoIP. Victimization encrypted VoIP technology, offenders will shield voice conversations from interception.

Techniques can even be combined. Victimization software package tools, offenders will inscribe messages and exchange them in photos or pictures – this technology is named steganography. For inquiring authorities, it is difficult to tell apart the harmless exchange of vacation photos and also the exchange of images with encrypted hidden messages.

The availability and use of encoding technologies by criminals may be a challenge for law-enforcement agencies. Varied legal approaches to handle the matter square measure presently underneath discussion, including potential obligations for software package developers to put in a back-door for law-enforcement agencies; limitations on key strength; and obligations to disclose keys, within the case of criminal investigations. However encoding technology isn't solely utilized by offenders – there square measure varied ways that such technology is employed for legal functions. While not adequate access to encoding technology, it's going to be tough to safeguard sensitive data. Given the growing variety of attacks, self-defense is associate in nursing necessary component of cybersecurity.

Hacking

Hacking is tagged as amongst the foremost serious of all cyber crimes. It's same that hacking erodes the religion of individuals in data technology and therefore the web. Hacking an ADP system has been projected as a menace requiring harsh laws to act as deterrents. Such a general projection is somewhat misconceived.

Hacking a pc merely implies entering into another's pc while not permission. Gaining unlawful access to another's pc is hacking. Unauthorized entry into a PC happiness to a different is hacking. It's appreciate phone-tapping. Hackers see the weakness within the target programme and so notice ways in which to enter and access in that. Anti-hacking tools such as the 'Firewall' technology and intrusion detection systems area unit preventive measures that may be taken to safeguard a pc from being hacked. Firewall, like a wall of the hearth, prevents hacking. Intrusion observation systems can additionally conjointly try and detect the supply of hacking.

Hacking perse, in straightforward terms, is criminal trespass into a pc that's a non-public property. Criminal trespass beneath the Indian legal code, 1860 is solely outlined as moving into the property within the possession of associate other with intent to commit an offense or to intimidate, insult or chafe associate in nursing such person or with intent to commit an offense.

Criminal trespass entails a penalization of imprisonment up to 3 months or fine up to rupees 5 hundred, or with both 97 Criminal trespass, the purse is so a minor offense.

Here may be a list of nice hackers of the planet;

The most renowned hacker in the history is Kevin Mitnick. At the tender age of seventeen in 1981, he hacked into a phone exchange that allowed him to airt subscriber calls in any method he wished. In 1983, he accessed a Pentagon pc. In the 1990s, he cracked/hacked/broke into the pc systems of the world's prime technology and telecommunications firms like Nokia, Fujitsu, Motorola and Sun Microsystems. He was inactive by the FBI in 1995 and later freed on parole in 2000. Gary McKinnon, Associate in Nursing Englishman, was inactive in Gregorian calendar month 2002 on the accusation that he had hacked into quite ninety US military pc systems within the U.K. Vladimir Levin, a Russian pc 'expert' is claimed to be the first to hack a bank to steal cash. In early 1995, he hacked into Citibank and robbed US$ ten million. He was inactive by international law enforcement agency within the U.K. in 1995, once he had transferred cash to his accounts within the US, Finland, Holland, Germany, and Israel.

Al. a. station declared a contest that may reward the 102nd caller with a 'Porsche 944S2'. Kevin Poulsen took management of the complete city's phone work and ensured he was the winner being the 102nd caller. He additionally hacked into 'Arpanet' that was the precursor to the web. Arpanet was a world network of computers.

US-based mostly hacker Timothy actor planted a malicious package code within the electronic network of Omega Engineering that was a major provider of elements to an independent agency and also the naval forces. Omega lost US$10 million because of the attack by that its producing operations were impaired.

Species of criminal trespass are treated with additional deterrent punishments. As an example, penalization for house-trespass is punishable with imprisonment up to one year. House-trespass so as to commit Associate in a Nursing offense punishable with death (i.e. murder etc.) is punishable with imprisonment for keeps or rigorous imprisonment up to 10 years. House-trespass so as to commit Associate in nursing offence punishable with imprisonment for keeps is punishable with imprisonment up to 10 years. House-trespass, aside from the on top of, entails penalization with imprisonment extending to 2 years and if the offense meant to be committed is thieving, the term of the imprisonment could be seven years. For house-trespass committed once preparation to cause hurt, assault or wrongful restraint or golf shot someone in such worry, the penalization prescribed is imprisonment extending to seven years. Lurking house-trespass or burglary is punishable with imprisonment extending to 2 years. Lurking house-trespass or house breaking Associate in nursing entering burglary so as to commit an offense punishable with imprisonment, is answerable for imprisonment up to 3 years and if such meant offense is thieving, the term of imprisonment has been extended to 10 years. The penalization for lurking house-trespass or burglary by night is punishable with imprisonment extending to 3 years. Grievous hurt caused while committing lurking house-trespass or housebreaking is punishable with imprisonment for life, or imprisonment extending to 10 years. All persons put together involved in lurking house-trespass or burglary by night, square measure liable to be censured with imprisonment for keeps or extending to 10 years, wherever death or grievous hurt is caused or tried to be caused by anyone or additional of them.

Another instance of associate in a nursing offense that has various species is "mischief". Each species of mischief is on an individual basis set down within the I.P.C. with differing punishments, relying upon the magnitude therefrom. Several of the offenses in the I.P.C. such as theft, criminal breaches of trust, cheating etc., have their individual species that square measure treated otherwise from each other. The legal approach towards hacking ought to be an equivalent as that of criminal trespass, mischief and also the innumerable alternative offenses within the I.P.C. All kinds of hacking cannot be treated alike. It must be understood that hacking to has various dimensions and species like alternative offenses.

A person World Health Organization enjoys exploring pc systems is additionally a hacker. Several teenagers enthusiastic about the web and computers hack for fun and excitement. Excitement to create a sway, show of capability and information of computers, fun and promotional material, and also the want to explore square measure a number of the motives of those teenagers to hack into pc systems. Another style of hacking is by web security firms, to check the pc systems of their shoppers and potential shoppers, to impress them and acquire business assignments of putting in place security systems for the shoppers.

Hacking is additionally committed to wreck the business of competitors and enemies. Disruption of a pc and denial of access to someone licensed to access any pc, square measure a number of the damages that will be caused by hacking. Hacking is additionally done to spy into others pc systems and for stealing information/data residing in this. Hacking is additionally used as a Weapon to commit alternative crimes such as cheating and misappropriation of funds electronically from the checking account of another.

Hacking is finished at the country level too. Frequently, Pakistani hackers are suspect of hacking Indian websites. For example, the website of SEBI (Stock Exchange Board of India) was hacked whereby a link to a sexy website was inserted.

Hack visits are protestors against governments or establishments / organizations, United Nations agency protest through hacking. For example, anti-globalization protests are created through hacking the website of the international organization.

There are thus varied species of hacking, in essence, it's the offense of criminal trespass. All varieties of hacking cannot so be treated alike. It's the intent, purpose, and consequences of hacking that confirm its gravity. A twelve year recent, who, for excitement and taking part in a prank enters restricted websites, shouldn't be treated as a national enemy. A terrorist group hacking into a protected system like the defence laptop systems to steal nuclear secrets, or a criminal syndicate hacking to embezzle Brobdingnagian amounts, cannot be treated on par with a young person prying into the laptop system of his best friend's girlfriend or even the CBI (Central Bureau of Investigation) for fun and excitement. The character of the hacking determines the gravity and all forms of hacking ought to not be projected or wrongfully treated within the same manner. Hacking has such a lot of species. Hacking could be an ability which will be used absolutely further as negatively. a person gap locks to assist folks that have lost the key's a Smith. However, someone United Nations agency opens locks to steal could be an outlaw.

The seriousness of hacking depends upon the character, purpose, intent and therefore the extent of loss and injury that are caused to the victim. For example, during a reportable incident within the U.S., the owner of a hobby website for youngsters received an e-mail informing her that a gaggle of hackers had gained management over her website. They demanded a ransom of 1 million bucks. The threat was unmasked as a mere scare plan of action. A number of days late, she discovered that the hackers had 'web-jacked' her website. 'Web-jacking' has been equated with hijacking an airplane, as forcibly assumptive management of a website, for various motives. The hackers had altered a region of the website that aforesaid "How to own fun with goldfish". The word "goldfish" was replaced with "piranhas". Piranhas are little however very dangerous flesh intake fish. Several youngsters visiting the website, purchased 'piranhas' from pet retailers and tried fiddling with them, thereby symptom themselves badly.

Hacking in varied forms is already a part of many offenses, either as the suggests that to their commission or as a consequence. For example, hacking might be a tool and suggests that to commit cheating, misappropriation, criminal breach of trust, theft, copyright violations, spying into official secrets, or as a part of the conspiracy to wage war against the State, that is all well-outlined offenses. A number of the species of hacking are outlined as contraventions further as criminal offenses within the LT. Act, 2000 as amended by the I.T. (Amendment) Act, 2008. Within the original version of the I.T. Act, 2000, section 66 outlined and reprimanded hacking within the following terms: "Hacking with ADP system - Whoever with the intent to cause or knowing that he's possible to cause wrongful loss or harm to the general public or any person destroys or deletes or alters any data residing in a laptop resource or diminishes its price or utility or affects it injuriously by any suggests that, commits hacking.

The title of the aforementioned section sixty-six was a name, that created confusion. It had been widely believed as if section sixty-six was the sole legal provision that handled the offense of hacking an ADP system. This confusion has been done away with, by sure amendments created by the I.T. (Amendment) Act, 2008. The words "Hacking with laptop System" are deleted from section sixty-six, the scope of that has been considerably widened:

"If someone, venally or fraudulently, will any act mentioned in section forty-three, he shall be punishable with imprisonment for a term which can be 3 years or with fine which can be 5 hundred thousand rupees or with both".

The various species of the offense of hacking that are provided (even though not referred to as 'hacking' specifically) for or could have components of hacking, within the amended version of the I.T. Act, 2000 are:

- Access to a laptop.

- Downloading, repetition or extraction of information from a laptop.

- Introducing computer program and contaminants.

- Causing harm to a laptop.

- Causing disruption of a laptop.

- Causing denial of access to a laptop.

- Affecting important data infrastructure.

- Cyber coercion.

Net Hijacking

Web hijacking suggests that taking forceful management of website of others. During this case, the owner of a website loses management over his website and its content.

Denial of Service Attack

Give Short for denial-of-service attack, a sort of attack on a network that's designed to bring the network to its knees by flooding it with useless traffic. Several DoS attacks, like the Ping of Death and Teardrop attacks, exploit limitations within the TCP/IP protocols. In a typical affiliation, the user sends a message asking the server to authenticate it. The server returns the authentication approval to the user. Find the user once it tries to send the authentication approval. The server waits, generally over a moment, before closing the affiliation. Once it will shut the affiliation, the wrongdoer sends a replacement batch of cast requests, and also the method begins once more docking the service indefinitely.

Attacks are often directed at any network device, together with attacks on routing devices and internet, electronic message, or name System servers. A DoS attack is often perpetrated during a range of the way. There square measure 3 basic forms of attack:

1. Consumption of machine resources like information measure, disc space or central processor Time;

2. Disruption of configuration data, such as routing information;

3. Disruption of physical network parts.

Distributed denial of service attack (DDoS) happens once multiple compromised systems flood the information measure or resources of a targeted system, typically one or additional internet servers. These systems square measure compromised by attackers employing a form of ways. Malware will carry DDoS attack mechanisms; one in every of the additional documented samples of this was MyDoom. Its DoS mechanism was triggered on a particular date and time. A system may additionally be compromised with a Trojan, permitting the wrongdoer to transfer a zombie agent. Attackers also can burgled systems mistreatment machine-driven tools that exploit flaws in programs that listen for connections from remote hosts. This situation primarily considerations systems acting as servers on the online. It's vital to notice the distinction between a DDoS and DoS attack. If Associate in nursing wrongdoer mounts a smurf attack from one host it might be classified as a DoS attack. In fact, any attack against availableness would be classed as a Denial of Service attack. On the alternative hand, if Associate in nursing wrongdoer uses, a thousand zombie systems to simultaneously launch smurf attacks against a far-off host, this is able to be classified as a DDoS attack.

The major benefits to associate in nursing wrongdoer of employing a distributed denial-of-service attack square measure that multiple machines will generate additional attack traffic than one machine, multiple attack machines square measure tougher to show off than one attack machine, and that the behavior of every attack machine will be stealthier, creating it tougher to trace down and stop working. Trinoo was the primary documented Distributed Denial of Service attack used against the University of MN in August 1999. However, the wrongdoer responded just by introducing new daemon machines into the attack. Trinoo was 1st found as a binary daemon on a variety of compromised Solaris a pair of.x systems. The malicious code had been introduced through the exploitation of buffer over-run bugs within the remote procedure decision (RPC) services.

Trojan attacks

A Trojan as this program is with competence referred to as is an associate unauthorized program that functions from within what appears to be a licensed program, thereby concealing what it's really doing.

There are several straightforward ways in which of putting in a Trojan in someone's laptop. Once the woman, asked to settle on, selected Mukesh over Rahul, Rahul set to urge even. On the14th of Gregorian calendar month, he sent Mukesh a spoofed e-card, that gave the impression to have returned from Radha's mail account. The e-card really contained a Trojan. As presently as Mukesh opened the cardboard, the Trojan was put in on his laptop. Rahul currently had complete management over Mukesh's laptop and proceeded to harass him totally.

Internet time thefts

This connotes the usage by an associate unauthorized person of the net hours purchased by another person. During a case reported before the enactment of the data Technology Act, 2000 commissioned military officer Bajwa, a resident of latest urban center, asked a close-by web café owner to return and started his net affiliation. For this purpose, cyber web café owner required to grasp his username and word. Once having started the affiliation he went away with knowing this username and word. He then sold this data to a different web café. One week later commissioned military officer Bajwa found that his net hours were nearly over. Out of the one hundred hours that he had bought,

94hours had been dried-up at intervals the span of that week. Surprised, he reported the incident to the urban center police. The police couldn't believe that point may well be taken. They weren't conscious of the thought of time-theft the least bit. Commissioned military officer Bajwa's report was rejected. He set to approach the days of India, New Delhi. They successively carried a report concerning the inadequacy of the capital of India Police in handling cyber crimes. The Commissioner of Police, urban center then took the case into his own hands and therefore the police below his directions raided and in remission cyber web café owner below the charge of thievery as outlined by the Indian legal code. Cyber web café owner spent many weeks barred up in Tihar jail before being granted bail.

Web jacking

This occurs once somebody forcefully takes management of an internet site (by cracking the word and later ever-changing it). The particular owner of website doesn't have any longer management over what seems thereon website. In aduring in associate exceedingly in a very recent incident reported within the USA the owner of a hobby website for youngsters received an e-mail informing her that a bunch of hackers had gained management over her website. They demanded a ransom of one million bucks from her. The owner, a teacher, didn't take the threat seriously. She felt that it had been simply a scare maneuver and unheeded the e-mail. It had been 3 days later that she came to grasp, following several phone calls from everywhere the country, that the hackers had net jacked her web site. Afterward, that they had altered a little of the website that was entitled 'How to own fun with goldfish'. Altogether the places wherever it had been mentioned, that they had replaced the word 'goldfish' with the word 'piranhas'. Piranhas are little however very dangerous flesh - intake fish.

Many youngsters had visited the popular website and had believed what the contents of the web site prompt. These unfortunate youngsters followed the directions, tried to play with piranhas, that they bought from pet retailers, and were terribly seriously slashed.

Theft of automatic data processing system

This type of offense involves the thievery of a laptop, some part(s) of a laptop or peripheral hooked up to the pc.

Physically damaging an automatic data processing system

This crime is committed by physically damaging a laptop or its peripherals.

Introduction :

Cybercrime may be a reasonably crime that happens in "cyberspace", that is, happens in the world of pc and, therefore, the web. Though

CYBERCRIME: Defeat Cybercrime with Awareness

many folks have a restricted information of "cybercrime", this sort of crime has the intense potential for severe impact on our lives and society, as a result of our society is turning into info society, full of info exchange happening in "cyberspace". Thus, it's necessary to introduce crime elaborate. whereas their area unit many textbooks talking regarding crime, however, that specialize in the statutes and laws relevant to this new breed of crime, few papers or textbooks concentrate on the "computer science" itself. In different words, most of the materials remark the "crime" of "cybercrime", however, this paper can speak additional regarding "cyber".

The term —cybercrime‖ may be a name. This term has obscurity been each embodies conduct whether or not act or omission, that cause a breach of rules of law and balanced by the sanction of the state. Before evaluating the conception of crime it's obvious that the conception of standard crime be mentioned and therefore the points of similarity and deviance between each these forms could also be mentioned.

The history of crime is brief compared with ancient crimes. The primary revealed report of crime occurred within the Nineteen Sixties, once computers were giant mainframe systems. Since mainframes weren't connected with different ones and solely few folks will access them, the cybercrimes were perpetual "insider" cybercrimes, which suggests employment allowed them to access into mainframe computers. Actually, in the Nineteen Sixties and Seventies, the crime, that was "computer crime" actually, was completely different from the crime we tend to featured with these days, as a result of no web in this era.

At an equivalent time, the crime wasn't solely restricted in target cybercrime, however, enlarged into tool crime and pc incidental. This method is comparable to the method of learning one language. In childhood, we learn the language itself; then, after we get older and area unit smart at it, we are going to use it to speak with one another, however, itself isn't a first-rate part. In general, current agreement on the classification of crime is to divide it into 3 classes that area unit same within the 1st paragraph on top of. we will set another analogy: target crime is like a crossword puzzle, that focuses on the magic of language itself; tool crime is comparable to fraud or harassment on street or in different face-to-face ways in which, however, the place during which tool crime happens isn't physical setting, however, cyberspace; pc incidental, as well as some electronic proof, is saved in pc or the camera captures the criminal retreating cash in an exceeding bank. Generally, these 3 classes area unit careful within the 3 following sections and in every section some latest cases are going to be studied.

Virus / worm attacks

Viruses are programs that attach themselves to a laptop or a file then flow into themselves to different files and to different computers on a network. They sometimes have an effect on the info on a laptop, either by neutering or deleting it. Worms, not like viruses don't want the host to connect themselves to. They just build purposeful copies of themselves and try this repeatedly until they eat up the whole available house on a computer's memory. The VBS_LOVELETTER virus (better called the Love Bug or the ILOVEYOU virus) was reportedly written by a Filipino undergrad. In 2000, this deadly virus beat the asterid dicot genus virus hollow - it became the world's most current virus. It smote one in every 5 personal computers within the world.

When the virus was brought beneath check actuality magnitude of the losses was incomprehensible.
The topic line and people United Nations agency had some data of viruses failed to notice the little. VBS extension and believed the file to be a computer file conquered individuals cautious of gap e-mail

attachments. The message within the e-mail was "kindly check the connected LOVELETTER coming back from me".

Since the initial occurrence over thirty variants of the virus is developed several of them following the initial by simply a number of weeks. Not like the as terid dicot genus virus this virus will have a harmful result. Whereas the as terid dicot genus, once put in, just inserts some text into the affected documents at a specific instant throughout the day, VBS_LOVELETTER initial selects sure files then inserts its own code in the position of the initial information contained within the file. This fashion creates ever- increasing versions of itself. In all probability, the world's most illustrious work was the net worm released on the net by financier someday in 1988. It took a team of consultants nearly 3 days to induce obviate the worm and within the meanwhile, several of the computers had to be disconnected from the network.

Virus Attacks

Viruses square measure the programs that have the aptitude to infect different programs and build copies of it and unfold into a different program. Programs that multiply like viruses, however, unfold from laptop to laptop square measure referred to as worms. These square measure malicious software system that attaches them to a different software system. Virus, worms, worm, Timebomb, Logic Bomb, Rabbit and microorganism square measure the malicious. Viruses typically have an effect on the info on a laptop, either by sterilization or deleting it. On the opposite hand worms simply build practical copies of them and try this repeatedly until they eat up all the out there. The worm could be a program that acts like one thing helpful however does the items that square measure quiet damping. Trojans are available in 2 components, a consumer half and a Server half. When the victim (unknowingly) runs the server on its machine, the offender can then use the consumer to attach to the Server and begin victimization the Trojan. TCP/IP protocol is that the usual protocol kind used for communications, however, some functions of the Trojans use the UDP protocol moreover.

Salami attacks

The key here is to build the alteration thus insignificant that in a single case it would go fully unnoted. E.g. a bank worker inserts a program, into the bank's servers, that deducts a tiny low quantity of cash (say Rs. five a month) from the account of each client. No account holder can in all probability notice this unauthorized debit, however, the bank worker can build a large quantity of cash monthly. To cite an associate degree example, associate degree worker of a bank in the USA was fired from his job. Discontent at having been purportedly beaten by his employers the person initial introduced a malevolent program into the bank's systems. Logic bombs programmes, that are activated on the incidence of a specific predefined event. The malevolent program was programmed to require 10 cents from all the accounts within the bank and place them into the account of the person whose name was alphabetically the last within the bank's rosters. Then he went associate degreed opened an account within the name of Ziegler. The number being withdrawn from every one of the accounts within the bank was thus insignificant that neither any of the account holders nor the bank officers noticed the fault. It absolutely was delivered to their notice once an individual by the name of Ziegler opened his account in this bank. He was stunned to search out a large quantity of cash being transferred into his account each Saturday.

Phishing

Offenders have developed techniques to get personal data from users, starting from spyware to "phishing" attacks. "Phishing" describes acts that square measure carried out to create victims disclose personal/secret data. Their square measure different types of phishing attacks, however, e-mail-based phishing attacks contain 3 major phases. Within the initial part, offenders determine legitimate firms giving online services and act electronically with customers whom they'll target, e.g. money establishments. Offenders style websites resembling the legitimate websites ("spoofing sites") requiring victims to perform traditional log in procedures, enabling offenders to acquire personal data (e.g. account numbers and online banking passwords).

In order to direct users to spoof sites, offenders send out e-mails resembling e-mails from the legitimate company, usually leading to trademark violations. The false e-mails raise recipients to log certain updates or security checks, generally with threats (e.g. to shut the account) if users do not get together. The false e-mail typically contains a link that victim ought to follow to the spoof website, to avoid users manually coming into the proper internet address of the legitimate bank. Offenders have developed advanced techniques to forestall users from realizing that they're not on the real website.

As presently as personal data is disclosed, offenders log in to victims' accounts and commit offenses like the transfer of cash, application for passports or new accounts, etc. The rising variety of winning attacks proves phishing's potential. Over 55000 distinctive phishing sites were according to APWG in April 2007. Phishing techniques aren't restricted to accessing passwords for online banking solely. Offenders may additionally get access codes to computers, auction platforms, and Social Security numbers, that square measure notably necessary within U.S. and might bring about to "identity theft" offenses.

Phishing and Vishing

In computing, phishing could be a sort of social engineering, characterized by makes an attempt to fraudulently acquire sensitive data, like passwords and MasterCard details, by masquerading as a trustworthy person or business in an apparently official electronic communication, such as an e-mail or an instant message. The term phishing arises from the employment of progressively refined lures to "fish" for 'users' monetary data and passwords. The e-mail directs the user to go to a web site wherever they're asked to update personal data, like passwords, MasterCard, social insurance, and checking account numbers, that the legitimate organization already has. The website, however, is phony and established solely to steal the user's data.

The motive behind phishing is that individuals can share their MasterCard information, passwords, checking account numbers and alternative data thinking that they're sharing their data to the legitimate organization, however, in reality, they're sharing their data with phony website or organization that goes to steal their cash.

Vishing is additionally alike phishing; it's the criminal follow of exploitation social engineering and phonation information science (VoIP) to realize access to non-public .personal and monetary data from the general public for the aim of economic reward. The term could be a combination of "voice" and phishing. Vishing exploits the public's trust in telephone circuit phone services, that have historically terminated in physical locations that area unit acknowledged to the phone company, and related toa bill-payer. The victim is usually unaware that VoIP permits for display spoofing, cheap, complicated machine-driven systems and obscurity for the bill remunerator. Vishing is often wont to steal MasterCard numbers or alternative data utilized in fraud schemes from people.

Misspelled URLs or the employment of subdomains area unit common tricks employed by phishers, as an example, the link http://www.google.com@membcrs.abc.com/ would possibly deceive an informal observer into basic cognitive process that the link can open a page on computer network.google.com, whereas the link really directs the browser to a page on members.abc.com, employing a username of computer network.google.com; were there no such user, the page would open usually. This methodology has since been closed off within the Mozilla and web human net browsers, whereas Opera provides a warning message and also the possibility to not follow the link.

Nowadays Phishing attacks are getting common sort of risk in Internet-based mostly Banking. Banks are for the most part forcing the shoppers to believe that the liability for Phishing ought to be borne by the customers as a result of they were negligent in responding to the Phishing mail. However, the legal position will be totally different. Phishing could be a result of multiple contraventions of knowledge Technology Act 2000 notably once the amendments of 2008. It ends up in a wrongful loss to the client. The dispute thus attracts provisions of Section forty-three for judgment. Already, many complaints are registered against Banks in an urban center, metropolis, and Hyderabad.

The Banks area unit primarily being command liable below the age previous Banking law that "Forgery can't be command against the client, but clever or undetectable the forgery is". To boot, Banks area unit ignoring the law of the land through IT Act 2000 furthermore because the pointers of run batted in and not exploitation digital signatures for authentication of web transactions. This makes them negligent below sections seventy-nine and eighty-five creating them answerable for any offense due to a laptop happiness to the Bank. Recently Bank of India has set precedence by acceptive liability for Phishing in one the cases filed in an urban center and repaying the number together with interest to the client UN agency was a victim of a Phishing fraud.

Cyber Stalking

Stalking generally suggests that the behavior of harassing or threatening the opposite person. Cyber Stalking is an extension of the physical style of stalking, that is committed to the new medium with the utilization of knowledge Technology. In cyber stalking the net, e-mail, chat rooms etc. area unit won't to stalk another person.

The Wikipedia defines cyberstalking, wherever the net or different electronic suggests that to stalk or harass a private, a gaggle of people, or a company. It embraces the creating of false accusations or statements of truth (as in defamation), monitoring, creating threats, fraud, injury to information or instrumentality, the solicitation of minors for sex, or gathering data that will be wont to harass.

Stalking may be a continuous method, consisting of a series of actions, each of which can be entirely legal in itself. The definition of Cyberstalking isn't universally acceptable because it varies place to put. In step with faculty member Lamber Royakkers -"Cyberstalking is that the repeatedly harassing or threatening of a private via the net or different electronic suggests that of communication. A cyberstalker is somebody with amorous and/or sexual motives United Nations agency perpetually harasses some other person electronically: via the bulletin board, chats box, email, spam, fax, buzzer or voice-mail. Stalking usually involves the constant harassment or threatening of somebody else: the following someone, showing at someone's house or work, creating harassing phone calls, feat written messages or objects, or vandalizing someone's property. As a result of the stalking activities area unit thus numerous and need to be seen in their association it's tough to convey an explicit description of stalking."

Cyberstalking doesn't involve any physical contact, however, stalking through the net has found favor among the offenders surely blessings offered like simple communication access to non-public data and obscurity.

As way as cyberstalking thinks about, the bad person has the advantage that he will sit anyplace within the world and harass the victim by posting bound disparaging comment or post comments on common discussion boards or place the mobile range of the victim and his email address on bound social sites that prompt the opposite users to send messages or phone calls to the victim in misconceived notion. The net has a wide reach, the method we have a tendency to communicate online, the private information of individual and different data is definitely accessed by the offenders through the net medium, and this makes the individual liable to the offense like cyberstalking.

Today net becomes the integral a part of one another life be it personal or career. The benefit of communication in today's world created it easier for the offenders or one who seeks to require revenge could use this medium to malign the victim by threatening and harassing by causation offensive emails. The very fact that cyberstalking doesn't involve physical contact could produce the misperception that it's a lot of benign than physical stalking. This can be not essentially true. because the net becomes an ever a lot integral a part of our personal and skilled lives, stalkers will benefit from the benefit of communications moreover as multiplied access to non-public data. Whereas a possible stalker could also be unwilling or unable to confront a victim in the flesh or on the phone, he or she could have very little hesitation causation harassing or threatening electronic communications to a victim. As with physical stalking, online harassment, and threats could also be a prelude to a lot of serious behavior, as well as physical violence.

Stalking has become a haul to girls and youngsters on a bigger half compared to men. Girls area unit vulnerable, vandalized, raped once it involves planet however constant things happen once cyberstalking takes place. Obscenity additionally adds up with the, threatens and harassment. Little doubt men additionally become the prey of constant, however, it's lower once it involves females. Youngsters additionally bear constant trauma from adult predators and pedophiles. The victim is generally someone United Nations agency is a smaller amount thorough concerning net services and its applications. The stalker is usually someone United Nations agency may be paranoid with no vanity. However, the traits disagree from one stalker to a different. Some harass to hunt revenge or thus me do so for his or her own pleasure. Whereas some simply to try to it for enjoying a mischief.

How do Cyber Stalkers operate?

a) If the stalker is one among the acquaintances of the victim he will simply get this data. If stalker could be an unknown to the victim, he collects the knowledge from the net resources like varied profiles, the victim might have crammed in whereas gap the chat or e-mail account or whereas sign language associate account with some website.

b) The stalker might post this data on any website associated with sex-services or qualitative analysis services, movement as if the victim is posting this data and invite the individuals to decide the victim on her phone numbers to own sexual services. Stalker even uses terribly filthy and obscene language to ask the interested persons.

c) Individuals of all kind from nook and corner of the globe, UN agency encounter this data, begin line the victim at her residence and/or workplace, posing for sexual services or relationships.

d) Some stalkers subscribe the e-mail account of the victim to countless sexy and sex sites, due to that victim starts receiving such reasonably uninvited e-mails.

e) Some stalkers continue causation recurrent e-mails posing for varied sorts of favors or threaten the victim.

f) In on-line stalking, the stalker will build the third party to harass the victim.

g) Follow their victim from the board to board. They stamping ground on identical as their victim, persistently posting notes to the victim, ensuring the victim is aware that he/she is being followed. Persistently they'll flame their victim (becoming eristic, insulting) to urge their attention.

h) Stalkers can nearly always build contact with their victims through email. The letters are also caressing, threatening, or sexually express. He can persistently use multiple names once contacting the victim.

i) Contact victim via phone. If the stalker is ready to access the victim phone, he persistently builds calls to the victim to threaten, harass, or intimidate them.

j) Track the victim to his/her home.

There unit 3 ways within which cyberstalking is conducted i.e.

1. **Stalking by E-mail -** wherever the bad person directly sends an e-mail to the victim to threaten her or to harass her. It's the foremost common style of stalking in the trendy world. The most common is causation have, obscene, sexy material and threatening mail to the victim.

2. **Stalking through the net –** this can be the international style of cyberstalking. During this the bad person doesn't invade the personal house of the victim, however, harasses her through the world medium in public. The bad person through the net medium post the phone numbers and email address of the victim on erotica sites and place morphed photos of the victim on the cyber house and threaten them. This can be the intense nature of cyberstalking wherever the stalker chases all the activity of the victim on Infobahn and announce false data regarding her on the websites.

3. **Stalking through laptop -** In this kind, the wrongdoer is a technocrat and he will lead of the laptop the pc of the victim as presently because the computer starts operative. During this, the stalker gets management of the victim's code and gets management over it. This type of cyberstalking needs high degree of laptop data to induce access to the targets laptop and therefore the choice out there to the victim is to disconnect the pc and abandon the present web address.

The term stalking isn't unaccustomed to the planet, within the physical house it existed for several centuries. The stalking within the physical world is finished by the previous friends, employees, or the one who desires to force his can over the target square measure the samples of stalkers. However, when the appearance of a computer network, the reach of the stalker is widened, he will reach to any a part of the planet and threaten and harass the target. It's not necessary currently to disclose his identity, most of the stalkers square measure the glum lover's, ex-boyfriends, colleagues, WHO did not satisfy their need and needs to harass the victim. Most stalkers square measure man and most victims square measure girls. The common reason behind the cyberstalking is rejection enamored or one-sided love, harassment, revenge, and show- off by the wrongdoer.

Following square measure the strategies used by the cyberstalker to target the victim:-

1. The stalker if he's an associate of the victim then he will gather all info the knowledge the data concerning the victim simply and if he's alien then he collects all info the knowledge the data through web from varied social network sites and collect all and each data concerning the victim from Date of birth, place of residence, place of labor, phone numbers, email ID's to places of visits everything.

2. The stalker could post all the data on any website associated with sex-services or chemical analysis services, and uses filthy and obscene language to ask person as if the victim himself denote these data that the interested person could decision the victim on his numbers to own sexual services.

3. All the folks from the planet would decision the victims on his phone numbers reception or on mobile posing for sexual services.

4. Some can send an e-mail to the victim attaching sexy material with it and generally denote these emails on the sexy sites.

5. Some can post morphed photos of the victim on these sexy and sex-service websites or keep posing for a favour and threaten them if

they are doing not fulfill their demands then they'll place these photos everywhere the web.

6. Generally the stalkers send them repetitive e-mails and decision them day and night at his phone numbers and keep track of them. The stalkers generally get the assistance of the third party to harass the victim.

The Social Networking sites like Facebook, Twitter, Orkut, Google and, Instagram and lots of a lot of are getting a medium to cyberstalking within the nowadays.

Punishment for the revelation of data in breach of lawful contract:

Save as otherwise provided during this Act or the other law for the nonce good, somebody as well as associates in nursing intermediator WHO, whereas providing services underneath the terms of lawful contract, has secured access to any material containing personal data concerning another person, with the intent to cause or knowing that he's seemed to cause wrongful loss or wrongful gain discloses, while not the consent of the person involved, or in breach of a lawful contract, such material to the other person shall be reproved with imprisonment for a term which can be 3 years, or with a fine which can be 5 hundred thousand rupees, or with each.

E-mail Bombing

In web usage, associate e-mail bomb may be a kind of web abuse consisting of causing immense volumes of e-mail to associate address in an effort to overflow the mailbox or overwhelms the server. Mail bombing is that the act of causing associate e-mail bomb, a term shared with the act of causing actual exploding devices. Mail bombing is generally accomplished by giving the victim's e-mail address to multiple spammers. Within the Russian web community, there is another sense for mail bomb. There, mail bomb may be a kind of denial of service attack against an ADP system.

E-mail bombing refers to causing an outsized range of e-mails to the victim leading to the victim's e-mail account(In case of Individual) or mail servers (in case of a corporation or associate in nursing e-mail service provider) blinking. In one case, a foreigner WHO had been residing in Shimla, Asian nation for pretty much thirty years wished to avail of a theme introduced by the Shimla Housing Board to shop for land at lower rates. Once he created Associate in nursing application it had been rejected on the grounds that the theme was accessible just for voters of the Asian nation. He determined to require his revenge. Consequently, he sent thousands of emails to the Shimla Housing Board and repeatedly unbroken causing e-mails until their servers crashed. E-mail bombing is characterized by abusers repeatedly causing associate in a nursing e-mail message to a selected address at a particular victim website. In several instances, the messages are giant and made from insignificant knowledge in a trial to consume extra system and network resources. Multiple accounts at the target website could also be abused, increasing the denial of service impact. E-mail spamming may be a variant of the bombing; it refers to causing e-mail to hundreds or thousands of users. E-mail spamming is created worse if recipients reply to the e-mail, inflicting all the first addressees to receive the reply.

E-mail Spoofing

E-mail spoofing may be a term won't to describe deceitful e-mail activity within which the sender address and alternative elements of the e-mail header square measure altered to appear as although the e-mail originated from a completely different supply. E-mail spoofing may be a technique ordinarily used for spam e-mail Associate in nursing phishing to cover the origin of an e-mail message. By ever-changing sure properties of the e-mail, like the From, Return-Path, and Reply-To fields (which is found within the message header), ill-intentioned users will create the e-mail seem to be from somebody aside from the particular sender. it's typically related to website spoofing that mimic associate in nursing actual, well-known, however, square measure go by another party either with deceitful intentions or as a method of criticism of the organization's activities."

It is the forgery of associate in nursing e-mail header in order that the message seems to possess originated from somebody or somewhere aside from the particular supply. Distributors of spam typically use spoofing in a shot to induce recipients to open, and probably even reply to, their solicitations. Spoofing is used lawfully. Classic samples of senders WHO would possibly like better to disguise the supply of the e-mail embody a sender reportage pattern by a relation to a welfare agency or a "whistle-blower" WHO fears revenge. However, spoofing anyone aside from you is against the law in some jurisdictions.

E-mail spoofing is feasible as a result of straightforward Mail Transfer Protocol (SMTP), the most protocol utilized in causing e-mail, doesn't embody associate in nursing authentication mechanism. Though Associate in Nursing SMTP service extension permits associate in nursing SMTP consumer to barter a security level with a mail server, this precaution isn't typically taken. If the precaution isn't taken, anyone with the requisite data will hook up with the server and use it to send messages. Anywhere, locution regardless of the sender needs it to mention. Thus, somebody may send a spoofed e-mail that seems to be from you with a message that you just didn't write.

Recently Flipkart business executive Binny Bansal's email account was spoofed. The Official statement from the corporate has declared that the CEO's e-mail account has been spoofed and therefore the spoofed email doesn't originate from the important supply however from a distinct supply determination the name associate in the nursing address with an ulterior motive. the corporate conjointly filed a police complained and free the statement that they need to file a case of email spoofing that involves the use of a cast email header to create it seem like a legitimate email. This case of email spoofing was directly detected and a report was filed with police.

Logic Bombs

In a worm, a malevolent program may be a programming code, inserted sneakily or by choice, that is designed to execute (or "explode") below circumstances like the lapse of a particular quantity of your time or the failure of a program used to retort to a program command. It's in result a delayed-action pc virus or Trojan horse. A logic bomb, when "exploded," could also be designed to show or print a spurious message, delete or corrupt knowledge, or produce other undesirable effects.

These square measure event dependent programs. This suggests that these programs square measure created to try and do one thing only a particular event (known as a trigger event) happens. E.g. even some viruses could also be termed logic bombs as a result of they lie dormant at some point of the year and become active solely on a selected date (like the Chernobyl virus).

Online gambling

There square measure immeasurable websites; all hosted on servers abroad, that provide online gambling. In fact, it's believed that a lot of those websites are literally fronts for hiding. Cases of banking system transactions and hiding over the net are reportable.

Knowledge Diddling

Data diddling involves dynamic knowledge previous or throughout input into a pc. In different words, data is modified from the method it ought to be entered by an individual typewriting within the knowledge, a virulent disease that changes knowledge, the computer programmer of the information or application, or anyone else concerned within the method of getting data to hold on in a very data file. The perpetrator may be anyone concerned with the method of creating; recording, encoding, examining, checking, converting, or transmittal knowledge. This can be one amongst the only strategies of committing a computer-related crime, as a result of it needs virtually no pc skills whatever. Despite the benefit of committing the crime, the value may be substantial.

Electricity co-operation area unit the one WHO principally suffer because of this type of crime in the Asian country. An assortment of cash, computerized accounting, record maintenance and remission within the bank were solely left to a personal contractor WHO was a pc skilled. The illegal immense quantity of funds by manipulating knowledge files to indicate less receipt and bank remission.

Sausage Attacks

A sausage attack is a series of minor knowledge security attack that that along end in a bigger attack. As an example, a fraudulent activity in a very bank, wherever associate worker steals a little number of funds from many accounts, can he thought-about a sausage attack. Crimes involving sausage attacks generally area unit difficult to notice and trace. These attacks area unit used for the commission of monetary crimes. The key here is to create the alteration therefore insignificant that in a very single case it'd go utterly unremarked. A bank worker inserts a program, into the bank's servers, that deducts a little quantity of cash (say Rs. five a month) from the account of each client. No account holder can in all probability notice this unauthorized debit, however, the bank worker can create a large quantity of cash each month.

To cite an associate example, an associate worker of a bank in the USA was discharged from his job. Dissatisfied at having been purportedly maltreated by his employers the person 1stintroduced a slag code into the bank's systems. The slag code was programmed to require 10 cents from all the accounts within the bank and place them into the account of the person whose name was alphabetically the family name of Karl Waldemar Ziegler. The quantity being withdrawn from every one of the accounts within the bank was therefore insignificant that neither the account holders nor the bank official noticed the fault. It had been delivered to their notice once an individual by the name of Karl Waldemar Ziegler opened his account therein bank. He was stunned to search out a large quantity of cash being transferred into his account each Sabbatum.

Web Time thievery

Theft of web hours refers to victimization someone else's web hours. Section 43(h) of the Indian Technology Act, 2000, lays down civil liability for this offense. It reads as, whoever while not the permission of the owner or the other one that is in charge of a pc, computing system or electronic network, charges the services availed of by someone to the account of another person by change of state with or manipulating any pc, computing system, electronic network is vulnerable to pay damages not surpassing one large integer to the person on workplace. Normally in these styles of thefts of the web, another person uses up surfing hours of the victim. This is often done by gaining access to the login ID and also the parole. E.g. commissioned military officer Bajwa's case this case rumored before the enactment of the knowledge technology Act, 2000. In could 2000, the economic offenses wing, IPR section crime branch of Old Delhi police registered its 1st case involving thievery of web hours. Bajwa's login name and parole from numerous places causing wrongful loss of one hundred hours to notch. Bajwa. Old Delhi police inactive the suspect for thievery of web time.

On additional inquiry within the case, it absolutely was found that Krishan Kumar, son of associate ex-officer, operating as senior Gov. in M/s Highpoint Tours & Travels had used notch Bajwa's login and passwords as several as 207 times from his residence and double from his workplace. He confessed that Shashi Nagpal, from whom he had purchased a pc, gave the login and parole to him. The police couldn'tbelieve that point can be taken. They weren't attentive to the construct of time-theft in the least. Commissioned military officer Bajwa's report was rejected. He set to approach the days of the Asian country, New Delhi. They successively carried a report regarding the inadequacy of the capital of India Police in handling cyber crimes. The Commissioner of Police, Old Delhi then took the case into his own hands and also the police underneath his directions raided and inactive Krishan Kumar underneath sections 379, 411, thirty-four of IPC and section twenty-five of the Indian Telegraph Act. In another case, the Economic Offences Wing of Old Delhi Police inactive a pc engineer World Health Organization got hold of the parole of an online user, accessed the pc and scarf 107 hours of web time from the opposite person's account. He was set-aside for the crime by an Old Delhi court throughout could 2000.

Cyber Defamation

When someone publishes calumnious matter regarding somebody on a website or sends e-mails containing calumnious data to any or all of that person friends, it's termed as cyber defamation.

Larceny of ADP system

This type of offense involves the larceny of a laptop, some part(s) of a laptop or a peripheral connected to the pc.

Forgery

Computers, printers, and scanners square measure won't to forge counterfeit currency notes, postage and revenue stamps, mark sheets etc. These square measure created victimization computers, and top quality scanners and printers.

Virus and Contaminants

Computer contaminants and virus have an extended history. Theories of self- replicating programs were initially developed in 1949. In 1981, Apple Viruses one, a pair of and three were found on Apple II operational systems. These viruses had unfolded through pirated pc games. In 1987, the 'Lehigh' virus infected the another kind of knowledge breach is a breach of trust with regard to knowledge and knowledge. The I.T. business primarily deals with knowledge and knowledge in some type or the opposite. A center uses knowledge to answer queries of consumers of banks, telecommunication service suppliers etc. A software system company develops a software system mistreatment knowledge and knowledge. A website compiles data and presents it online.

Data and knowledge drive the I.T. industry. They're the inputs, stuff, and outputs for the I.T. industry. Knowledge and knowledge are also entrusted to workers of the organization, its business associates, service suppliers, agents and different parties for specific functions. Incidents of breach of knowledge and knowledge, by such trustworthy parties of times confront the I.T. industry. Misappropriation knowledge of data / information by an individual WHO holds it in trust would quantity to criminal breach of trust underneath the Indian legal code.

Limited had derived Just Dial information onto its freshly launched website: web.askme.in, thereby violating Just Dial's information copyrights. The injunction was granted expert by the Hon'ble judicature and additional order has been created for search and seizure to be dispensed at Infomedia's urban center and Bombay offices, as the prima-facie case, was created out by the simply Dial officers.

E-commerce/ Investment Frauds

Merchandise or services that were purchased or shrunk by people online are ne'er delivered. The fraud as a result of the untruth of a product publicized purchasable through a web auction web site or the non-delivery of merchandise purchased through a web auction site. Investors are enticed to take a position during this racket by the guarantees of abnormally high profits.

Knowledge thievery

The biggest case of knowledge breach/data thievery/identity theft was exposed in Gregorian calendar month, 2009, during which Albert Gonzalez, a 28-year-old Yankee alongside his 2 Russian accomplices,

94

were inactive for masterminding an international theme to steal knowledge of over a hundred thirty million credit and debit cards by hacking into the pc systems of 5 major firms together with Hannaford Bros Supermarkets, 7-Eleven and region Payment Systems, a MasterCard process company.145 Gonzalez has been the same to be one in every of the nation's (U.S.) cyber-crime kingpins, by prosecutors. Previously, he was alleged to be the kingpin WHO masterminded a knowledge breach of over forty million credit card numbers from TJX Cos et al., inflicting the parent company of TJ Maxx chain, losses of concerning US$ two hundred million.

Hacking is completed at the country level too. Frequently, Pakistani hackers square measure suspect of hacking Indian websites. As an example, the website of SEBI (Stock Exchange Board of India) was hacked whereby a link to a sexy website was inserted. Hack square measure protestors against governments or establishments / organizations, United Nations agency protest through hacking. As an example, anti-globalization protests are created through hacking the website of WTO.

There square measure so varied species of hacking, although, in essence, it's the offense of criminal trespass. All sorts of hacking cannot so be treated alike. It's the intent, purpose, and consequences of hacking that verify its gravity. A twelve year previous, who, for excitement and taking part in a prank enters restricted websites, mustn't be treated as a national enemy. A FTO hacking into a protected system like the defence pc systems to steal nuclear secrets, or a criminal syndicate hacking to steal vast amounts, can't be treated on par with a youngster prying into the pc system of his best friend's girlfriend or even the CBI (Central Bureau of Investigation) for fun and excitement. The character of the hacking determines the gravity and all forms of hacking ought to not be projected or lawfully treated within the same manner. Hacking has such a big amount of species. Hacking could be a talent which will be used completely similarly as negatively. A person gap locks to assist those that have lost the key's a Smith. However, someone United Nations agency opens locks to steal could be a malefactor.

The seriousness of hacking depends upon the character, purpose, intent and also the extent of loss and injury that square measure caused to the victim. As an example, in a very rumored incident within the U.S., the owner of a hobby website for youngsters received AN e-mail informing her that a bunch of hackers had gained management over her website. They demanded a ransom of 1 million greenbacks. The threat was unmasked as a mere scare plan of action. A couple of days late, she discovered that the hackers had 'web-jacked' her website. 'Web-jacking' has been equated with hijacking a plane, as forcibly presumptuous management of a website, for numerous motives. The hackers had altered a district of the website that same "How to own fun with goldfish". The word "goldfish" was replaced with "piranhas". Piranhas square measure small however very dangerous flesh intake fish. Several kids visiting the website, purchased 'piranhas' from pet retailers and tried fidgeting with them, thereby symptom themselves badly.

Hacking in varied forms is already a part of many offenses, either as the means that to their commission or as a consequence. as an example, hacking may well be a tool and means that to commit cheating, misappropriation, criminal breach of trust, theft, copyright violations, spying into official secrets, or as a part of the conspiracy to wage war against the State, that square measure all well-outlined offenses. A number of the species of hacking are outlined as contraventions similarly as criminal offenses within the I.T. Act, 2000 as amended by the I.T. (Amendment) Act, 2008.

Virus and Contaminants

Computer contaminants and virus have a protracted history. Theories of self- replicating programs were 1stdeveloped in 1949. In 1981, Apple Viruses one, two and three were found on Apple II operative systems. These viruses had unfolded through pirated laptop games. In 1987, the 'Lehigh' virus infected the 'command.com' laptop files. In 1988, one in all the foremost common viruses,

'Jerusalem' was unleashed. This virus was activated each Fri the thirteenth and affected each '.exe' and '.com' files and deleted any programs run thereon day. In 1992, it had been discovered that 1300 viruses were breathing, that was a rise of 420% from Dec 1990. This was the year once the 'Dark attacker Mutation Engine' (DAME) was created, that was a toolkit that turned viruses into polymorphic viruses. In 1994, the 'Good Times' e-mail hoax molding through the pc community. The hoax warns of a malicious virus that might erase a whole hard-drive simply by gap associate degree e-mail with the topic line "Good Times". In 1995, 'Word Concept' became one in all the foremost current viruses, that unfold through Microsoft Word documents. In 1996, the 'Baza',

'Leroux' and 'Staog' viruses infected Windows ninety-five files, surpass and Linux severally. In 1998, 'Strange Brew' was the first virus to infect Java files. This year, the 'Chernobyl' virus additionally unfold quickly via '.exe' files. The virus was quite harmful, offensive not solely files however additionally the chip inside infected computers.

In 1999, the 'Melissa' virus infected regarding 1,000,000 computers. Also, 'Bubble Boy' was the first worm that didn't rely upon the recipient gap associate degree attachment for the infection to occur. As presently because the user opened the e-mail, the worm started its destruction. This year, 'Tristate' was the primary multi-program macro virus to be deployed and it infected Word, surpass and outlet files. Within the year 2000, the notable 'Love Bug', additionally referred to as the 'I LOVE YOU' virus increased itself via the Outlook program. The virus came as associate degree attachment and deleted files as well as 'MP3', 'MP2' and 'JPG'. It additionally sent usernames and passwords to the author of the virus. Also, the 'W97M.Resume.A', like the genus Melissa virus, infected 'Outlook' and unfold itself. In contrast to the previous viruses, 'Stages' was hidden in associate degree attachment with a false '.txt' extension, luring recipients to welcome it. The year 2000 was additionally the year once the 'distributed denial-of-service' attacks knocked out leading websites like 'Yahoo', 'eBay', 'Amazon' etc, for many hours. Shortly when the '9/11' attacks in 2001, the 'Nimda' virus infected many thousands of computers within the world. This virus has been amongst the foremost refined ones, with 5 totally different ways of replicating and infecting laptop systems. The 'Anna Kournikova' virus armored itself to individuals noncommissioned the victim's Microsoft Outlook address book. Many worms were additionally born this year like 'Sircam', 'CodeRed' and 'BadTrans'.

'Sircam' unfold personal documents over the web through e-mail, while 'Code Red' attacked vulnerable web-pages. It infected regarding 359,000 computers within the first twelve hours some. 'BadTrans' captured passwords and MasterCard info. In 2002, the creator of the 'Melissa' virus, David C. Smith was sentenced to twenty months within the federal jail. Many viruses named when celebrities like 'Shakira', 'Britney Spears' and 'Jennifer Lopez' additionally fold throughout this year. In 2003, the 'Slammer' worm, the quickest spreading worm until date, infected regarding 75000 computers in 10 minutes. This year, the 'Sobig' worm became amongst the first few worms to create the infected laptop systems spam relay points. In the year 2004, a laptop worm referred to as 'MyDoom' or 'Novarg' unfold through e-mails and file-sharing package quicker than its earlier cousins. 'MyDoom' enticed e-mail recipients to open associate degree attachment that allowed hackers to access the hard-drive of the afflicted computing system. The target of the worm was to create a 'denial of service' attack on the 'SCO Group' that was suing numerous teams for mistreatment associate degree open- supply version of its 'Unix' artificial language. SCO offered an award folks $2, 50,000 to anyone giving info leading to the arrest and conviction of the worm's authors. Also, the 'Sasser' Worm affected regarding 1,000,000 computers mistreatment Windows. Associate degree 18-year-old German high faculty-student confessed to developing this worm. The year 2005 'welcomed' the world's first cell-phone virus referred to as 'Common warrior-A'. It's aforesaid to own originated from Russia, spreading through a text message. Within the year 2008, the 'Conficker' virus infected between 9 and fifteen million laptop server systems across the globe, as well as servers of the French Navy, the U.K. Ministry of Defence, Norwegian Police and different giant government organizations.

A computer virus is as common because of the respiratory disease. Each laptop even that of an adult male. Bill Gates, the creator of Microsoft would suffer from a computer program at some purpose of your time or different. even as some dirt and insects square measure probably to creep into the house howsoever several precautions square measure taken, computer program should get into the pc through a CD, floppy or pen-drive that's corrupted or through the web wherever they float like their cousins within the air that cause respiratory disease, infectious agent fever or a lot of serious diseases. Section 43-(c) of the I.T. Act, 2000 imposes a financial liability of up to rupees one large integer upon someone World Health Organization, while not the permission of the owner or in charge of a laptop, introduces or causes to be introduced any laptop contamination or computer program into any laptop, computing system or electronic network Computer contaminant" means that any set of laptop directions that square measure designed-

• To change, destroy, record, transmit information or programme residing inside a laptop, computing system or laptop network; or

• By any means that to usurp the conventional operation of the pc, a computer system, or laptop network;

Section forty-three imposes a strict liability upon the one who plants any worm or material. All the violations stipulated in section forty-three together with clause (c) that covers the violation of introduction or inflicting the introduction of any laptop material or laptop virus into any laptop, have conjointly been created criminal offenses. Hence, deceitfully or fraudulently introducing or inflicting the introduction of a worm or laptop material into another's laptop, would conjointly represent a criminal offense entailing Associate in the Nursing imprisonment of 2 years. Even with preparation, to penalize the introduction of laptop material or virus into another's laptop, within the gift state of data technology in our country, is completely unreasonable. Our law manufacturers ought to have a minimum of asked themselves sure elementary queries before criminalizing the planting of worm and contaminants:-

• What's the extent of general awareness in our country concerning laptop contaminants and virus?

• What number folks in our country, WHO use computers, are tuned in to anti-virus software package and the way several out of them use the same?

• What is the general level of consciousness amongst folks, that before causation a data file to a different through a CD, floppy, pen-drive or the net, it ought to be checked whether or not there's a virus in it or not?

• With laptop contaminants and virus floating everyplace in floppies, CDs, pen-drives and therefore the net, however can or not it's proved clear or otherwise, on WHO introduced/transmitted the contaminants or virus in question?

• Our enforcement agencies and the judiciary equipped to see the supply of the pc material and virus?

It is very tough to search out the supply of an outbreak and material in an exceeding laptop system. The offense of planting virus and material in a computer system is vulnerable to gross misuse and incorrect application. The author of an outbreak and material, WHO infects multiple laptop systems, like the viruses and worms, mentioned higher than, would stand on a totally different footing. A harsh liability together with penalization, on the author of an outbreak that's circulated by him, is excusable. However, to prosecute persons WHO simply transmit virus and contaminants is an ex-facie lawgiver. There's hardly any awareness in our country concerning worm and contaminants or anti-virus software package. Our enforcement agencies don't have any experience to see the precise supply of the virus. It's much terribly tough to find the supply of an outbreak, particularly with viruses and contaminants floating in the cyber world like mud, and the virus that causes the common cold. Our legislators have to be compelled to have formed numerous different things and issues. For example, someone might not even grasp that there's a virus in his laptop. New sorts of virus acquire existence from time to time and lots of them aren't detectable by anti-virus software package. Hence, albeit someone installs anti-virus software package, the virus will creep into the pc and unwittingly such virus will be transmitted to others. Since intention/ men's real is inferred from the incident and its consequences, except the allegations by the litigator, false and misconceived criminal cases alleging planting virus and contaminants are doubtless to be galore in our country. Adding insult to injury, it'd be solely at the top of the ordeal of facing prosecution-cum-persecution, that the defendant would get a chance to prove his innocence throughout defense proof.

To make transmission of virus and contaminants, a criminal offense, ought to have waited for our folks to mature as users of computers and therefore the net, which might take a minimum of another fifteen to twenty years. A nominal fine sort of a traffic challan, to begin with, would have sufficed and therefore the law ought to have evolved with the expansion of awareness, consciousness, and maturity amongst laptop users at the giant. Transmission of virus or material, as a civil violation below section forty-three of the IT Act, 2000 with a nominal fine remains excusable.

However, handling the law because it is, an important responsibility lies on our judiciary to guard voters against harassment of being concerned for transmittal worm and contaminants. It'd be a tragic comedy to envision each person within the country because the complainant/victim of laptop contaminants and virus, and conjointly a criminal being defendant of introducing worm and/or contaminants into another's laptop.

PC information

The increasing use of engineering as well as the trend to medical aid of information light-emitting diode to an increasing relevancy of pc information. As a consequence pc information has become a frequent target of attacks that vary from information interference to information spying. Varied regional frameworks contain definitions for pc information. One example is section three of the Commonwealth Model Law on and Computer-related Crime.

Definitions;

During this Act, unless the contrary intention appears:

"computer data" means that any illustration of facts, info or ideas in a very type appropriate for the process in a very computing system, as well as a program appropriate to cause a computing system to perform a function;

The similar definitions square measure contained within the 2001 Council of Europe Convention on law-breaking, the 2005 EU Council Framework call on attacks against info systems, 2008 Draft ECOWAS Directive on Fighting Cyber Crime, and also the 2009 HIPCAR Model Legislative Text on law-breaking.

PC information device

Storage devices play a vital role with relevance law-breaking – each with relevance attainable information interference in addition like relevance the seizure of proof. One example for a regional framework that contains a definition is section three if the Commonwealth Model Law on pc and Computer-related Crime.

Definitions

"Computer information storage medium" means that any article or material (for example, a disk) from that information is capable of being reproduced, with or while not the help of the other article or device;

A similar definition is contained in HIPCAR Model Legislative Text.

Computing system

In law-breaking laws, the term computing system is employed in regard to substantive legal code in addition as procedural law. PC systems will be the target of an attack; they will be used as a tool once committing against the law and eventually will be appropriated as proof. Consequently, most applicable regional frameworks and model laws contain such a definition. One example is section three of 2002 Commonwealth Model Law on pc and Computer-related Crime.

Definitions

"Computer system" means that a device or a cluster of inter-connected or connected devices, as well as the web, one or a lot of that, consistent to a program, performs the automatic process of information or the other function;

One uncommon side is that the proven fact that the definition mentions "the Internet". The web is wide-out lined as a system of interconnected networks. From a technical perspective the web itself is thus not a computing system, however, a network and may consequently not be enclosed within the definition of, however, is also enclosed within the definition of pc networks. However, many drafters of legal frameworks followed the instance of the Commonwealth Model Law and enclosed the web within the definition of the computing system.

Definitions also are contained within the 2001 Council of Europe Convention on law-breaking, the 2005 EU Council Framework call on attacks against info systems, 2008 Draft ECOWAS Directive on Fighting Cyber Crime, and also the 2009 HIPCAR Model Legislative Text on law-breaking.

Pornography

At that point, the commercial pornography market targeted principally on Europe and also the United States and also the material was locally made, high-priced and tough to get. Approaches to shop for or sell pornography entailed a number of risks that now not – or a minimum of not a degree – exist these days. Within the past, producers failed to have the aptitude to develop photography and films. They were enthusiastic about services offered by businesses, that accumulated the possibilities of law-enforcement agents distinctive kid porn through reports from businesses handling the event. The provision of video cameras modified this case for the primary time. However, the risks weren't solely associated with production. Obtaining access to pornography was equally fraught with risks for the wrongdoer. Orders were placed by responding to advertisements in newspapers. Means that of communication between merchant and collector, and thus the market itself was restricted.

The situation changes dramatically with the provision of Internet-based data-exchange applications. Whereas within the past, enforcement was confronted with the analog material, these days the overwhelming majority of the discovered material is digital. Since the mid-1990s, offenders have progressively used network services for the distribution of such material. The ensuing issues in terms of police work and investigation child-pornography cases are acknowledged. The web is these days the most channel for commercialism regular porn still as pornography.

Several reasons for the shift from analog to digital distribution may be known. The web offers less technically skilled users the impression they will act invisibly from others. If the wrongdoer doesn't use anonymous communication technology, this impression is incorrect. However the actual fact that victimization subtle means that of anonymous communication will hinder the identification of the wrongdoer could be a matter of concern in respect of the exchange of kid porn online. Additionally, this development has been supported by the decreasing value of technical devices and services used for the assembly and commercialism of kid porn, like recording instrumentation and hosting services. Since websites and web services square measure receptive around 2 billion web users, the amount of potential customers has additionally swollen. There square measure issues that the actual fact that access is less complicated attracts folks that wouldn't have taken the danger of being caught attempting to get pornography outside the web. With the shift from analog to digital media, associate increasing range of child-pornography pictures discovered through investigations was reported. Another facet that in all probability supported this development is that the undeniable fact that digital data will normally be duplicated while not a loss of quality. Whereas within the past shoppers of kid porn wants to duplicate and trade the fabric was hindered by the loss in quality from the replica, these days a downloaded file will become the supply for additional duplications. one in all the implications of this development is that even once the wrongdoer United Nations agency made the fabric within the 1st place is in remission and his files square measure seized, it becomes tough to "remove" files once they need to be been listed over the web.

International organizations square measure engaged in the fight against online pornography, with many international legal initiatives, including the 1989 United Nations Convention on the Rights of the Child; 2003 European Union Council Framework call on combating the sexual exploitation of kidren of youngsters of kids and child pornography; and also the 2007 Council of Europe Convention on the Protection of kids against Sexual Exploitation and statutory offense, among others.

Sadly, these initiatives seeking to regulate the network distribution of porn have tested very little deterrent to perpetrators, United Nations agency uses the web to speak and exchange pornography. Arise in information measure has supported the exchange of flicks and movie archives.

Research into the behaviour of kid of kid porn offenders shows that fifteen per cent of in remission folks with Internet-related child porn in their possession had additional than 1000 footage on their computer; eighty per cent had footage of kids aged between half dozen and twelve years on their computer; nineteen per cent had footage of kids younger than the age of 3; and twenty-one per cent had footage depiction violence.

The sale of kid porn is very profitable, with collectors willing to pay nice amounts for movies and footage depiction youngsters during a sexual context. Search engines notice such material quickly.

Most material is changed in password-protected closed forums, that regular users and law- social control agencies will seldom access. Surreptitious operations square measure therefore very important in the fight against pornography.

The Internet is being extremely used as a medium to sexually abuse youngsters. The kids are viable victim to the law-breaking. Computers and net have become a necessity of each unit, the kids have gotten a straightforward access to the web. There's a straightforward access to the sexy contents on the web. Pedophiles lure the kids by distributing sexy material then they struggle to satisfy them for sex or to require their nude pictures as well as their engagement in sexual positions. Generally, pedophiles contact youngsters in the chat rooms sitting as teenagers or a toddler of comparable age then they begin changing into friendlier with them and win their confidence. Then slowly pedophiles begin sexual chat to assist youngsters shed their inhibitions concerning sex then decision them out for private interaction. Then starts actual exploitation of the kids by giving them some cash or incorrectly promising them sensible opportunities in life. The pedophiles then sexually exploit the kids either by victimization them as sexual objects or by taking their sexy photos so as to sell those over the web.

How do they operate?

a) Pedophiles use a false identity to entice the children/teenagers.

b) Pedophiles contact children/teens in varied chat rooms that are utilized by children/teen to move with different children/teen.

c) Tie the child/teen.

d) Extract personal info from the child/teen by winning his confidence.

e) Gets the e-mail address of the child/teen and starts creating contacts on the victim's e-mail address?

f) Starts causing sexy images/text to the victim as well as kid pornographic pictures so as to assist the child/teen shed his inhibitions so a sense is formed within the mind of the victim that what's being fed to him are traditional which everyone will it.

g) Extract personal info from child/teen.

h) At the tip of it, the pedophiles created a gathering with the child/teen out of the house then drag him into the net to additional sexually assault him or to use him as a soul.

Two key factors within the use of ICTs for the exchange of kid porn act as obstacles to the investigation of those crimes:

1 the utilization of virtual currencies and anonymous payment

Cash payment permits consumers of bound merchandise to cover their identity, thus money is dominant in several criminal businesses. The demand for anonymous payments has a light-emitting diode to the event of virtual payment systems and virtual currencies enabling anonymous payment. Virtual currencies might not need identification and validation, preventing law-enforcement agencies from tracing cash flows back to offenders. If such anonymous currencies square measure used by criminals it restricts the ability of enforcement to establish suspects by following cash transfers— for example in cases connected to business kiddie porn.

Erotic or sexy material (excluding kid pornography)

The sexually-related content was among the primary content to be commercially distributed over the web, that offers benefits to retailers of titillating and sexy material including:

• Exchange of media (such as footage, movies, live coverage) while not the requirement for cost-intensive shipping;

• Worldwide access, reaching a considerably larger range of consumers than retail shops;

• The web is commonly viewed as associate anonymous medium (often erroneously) – a side that customers of porn appreciate, visible of prevailing social opinions.

Recent analysis has known as several as four.2 million sexy websites that will be accessible on the web at any time. Besides websites, the sexy material may be distributed through file-sharing systems and instant electronic messaging systems.

Different countries criminalize titillating and sexy material to completely different extents. Some countries allow the exchange of sexy material among adults and limit lawmaking to cases wherever minors access this type of fabric, seeking to safeguard minors. Studies indicate that kid access to sexy material might negatively influence their development. To befits these laws, "adult verification systems" are developed. Different countries criminalize any exchange of sexy material even among adults, while not specializing in specific teams (such as minors).

For countries that criminalize interaction with the sexy material, preventing access to the sexy material could be a challenge. On the far side of the web, authorities will in several instances sight and prosecute violations of the prohibition of sexy material. On the web, however, as the sexy material is commonly pronto accessible on servers outside the country, social control is tough. Even wherever authorities square measure able to establish websites containing sexy material, they'll have not any powers to enforce the removal of offensive content by suppliers.

The principle of national sovereignty doesn't typically allow a rustic to hold out investigations among the territory of another country, while not permission from native authorities. Even once authorities look for the support of nations wherever offensive websites square measure hosted, roaring investigation and criminal sanctions are also hindered by the principle of "dual criminality".

To prevent access to sexy content, countries with exceptionally strict laws square measure typically restricted to interference (such as filter technology) to limit access to surf websites.

Erotic or sexy material

The legislating and gravity of legislating of extrajudicial content and sexually-explicit content varies between countries. The parties that negotiated the Council of Europe Convention on law-breaking targeted on the harmonization of laws concerning kiddy porn and excluded the broader legislating of sexy and sexy material. Some countries have addressed this drawback by implementing provisions that criminalize the exchange of sexy material through pc systems. However, the dearth of normal definitions makes it tough for law-enforcement agencies to research those crimes, if offenders act from countries that haven't criminalized the exchange of sexual content.

Examples;

One example of the legislating of the exchange of sexy material in Section 184 of the German legal code.

Section 184 Dissemination of sexy Writings

(1) Whoever, in regard to sexy writings (Section eleven segment (3)):

1. Offers or makes them accessible to an individual underneath eighteen years of age;

2. Displays, posts, present or otherwise makes them accessible at an area accessible to persons underneath eighteen years aged, or into that, they will see;

3. Offers or offers them to a difference in retail trade outside of the business premises, in kiosks or alternative sales areas that the client sometimes doesn't enter, through a mail-order business or in industrial disposal libraries or reading circles;

3a. Offers or offers them to a different by means that of industrial of economic of business rental or comparable commercial furnishing to be used, aside from retailers that aren't accessible to persons underneath eighteen years aged and into that they can't see;

4. Undertakes to import them by means that of a mail-order business;

5. In public offers, announces or commends them at an area accessible to persons underneath 18 years aged or into that they will see, or through the dissemination of writings outside of business transactions through traditional trade outlets;

6. Permits another to get them while not having been requested to try and do by him;

7. Shows them at a public film showing for compensation requested utterly or preponderantly for this showing;

8. Produces, obtains, supplies, stocks, or undertakes to import them so as to use them or copies made from them among that means of numbers one through seven or to form such use attainable by another; or

9. undertakes to export them so as to pass around them or copies made of them abroad in violation of the applicable penal provisions there or to form them in public access or to form such use attainable, shall be penalized with imprisonment for no more than one year or a fine.

This provision relies on the idea that trade and different exchange of sexy writings shouldn't be criminalized if minors aren't concerned. On this basis, the law aims to shield the undisturbed development of minors. Whether or not access to creation features a negative impact on the event of minors is arguable and far mentioned. The exchange of sexy writings among adults isn't criminalized by Section 184. The term "writing" covers not solely ancient writings, however additionally digital storage. Equally, creating them "accessible" not solely applies to acts on the far side of the web, however, covers cases wherever offenders create sexy content offered on websites.

One example of an approach that goes on the far side this and criminalizes any sexual content is Section four.C.1, Philippines draft House Law Bill No. 3777 of 2007.

Sec. 4.C1.: **Offenses associated with sexual arousal –** while not prejudice to the prosecution below Republic Act No.9208 and Republic Act No. 7610, someone WHO in any manner advertises, promotes or facilitates the commission of sexual arousal through the employment of knowledge and engineering like however not restricted to computers, pc networks, television, satellite, mobile phone,

Section 3i.: **Sexual arousal or Virtual Sex –** refers to any kind of gender or arousal with the help of computers or communications network this provision follows a really broad approach because it criminalizes any quite sexual advertisement or facilitation of gender administered over the web. Because of the principle of twin guilt, international investigations with respect to such broad approaches run into difficulties.

Porno

The Internet is turning into the most instruments for the trade and exchange of fabric containing porno. The foremost reasons for this development area unit the speed and potency of the web for file transfers, its low production and distribution prices and perceived obscurity. Footage placed on a webpage is accessed and downloaded by a lot of users worldwide. one amongst the foremost vital reasons for the "success" of web pages giving creation or perhaps porno is that the incontrovertible fact that net users feel less determined whereas sitting in their home and downloading material from the web. Unless the users have used means that of anonymous communication, the impression of no traceability is wrong. Most net users area unit merely unaware of the electronic path they leave whereas surfboarding.

The provisions criminalizing porno area unit designed generally to shield totally different legal interests. Lawmaking of the assembly of kid creation seeks to shield youngsters from falling victim to statutory offense. With respect to the prohibition of acts associated with the exchange of kid creation (offering, distributing) in addition as possession, lawmaking is meant to destroy the market, in so far as current demand for brand spanking, new material may encourage offenders to continue the abuse of youngsters. Additionally, the prohibition of exchange seeks to create it tougher for individuals to realize access to such material and thereby forestall a trigger result on the statutory offense of youngsters. Finally, lawmaking of possession intends to forestall offenders from victimization child-pornography material to seduce youngsters into obtaining concerned in gender.

Cyber Crimes associated with Finance

The Price Waterhouse Cooper's organization, that deals with the economic crime survey, has outlined economic crime in the cyber world as "an economic crime committed victimization computers and therefore the net. It includes distributing viruses, lawlessly downloading files, phishing and pharming, and stealing personal info like checking account details. It's solely a cybercrime if a laptop, or computers, and therefore the net play a central role in the crime, associate in nursing, not an incidental one."

According to the findings of a survey on Economic Crime in Bharat in Global Economic Crime Survey 2011. The employment of the net in Bharat is growing speedily. In line with a recent telecommunication regulatory agency of Bharat (TRAI) survey, we have a tendency to presently have 354 million net subscribers. whereas burgeoning growth within the use of net provides multiple choices to cyber voters all told potential spheres from recreation to education, it's conjointly given rise to cybercrime. This new breed of tech-savvy fraudsters poses a replacement set of challenges. Pure gold of the respondents, WHO rumored economic crime, have old cybercrime within the last twelve months. We have a tendency to believe that this knowledge alone shows however serious the chance of cybercrime is to organizations. Within the background of the recent incidents of cybercrime on international corporations and monetary establishments, a larger range of organizations has become victims of cybercrime. One potential reason that will justify this sudden rise in cybercrime is that the rise in the volume of e-business, larger penetration of net and e-commerce.

Economic crime doesn't discriminate. It's the real world. No business or organization is immune. We've seen that despite fraud being a heavy business issue, 100% of the respondents in 2011 as compared to six in 2009 wasn't aware of their organization has been a victim to economic crime within the last twelve months. The explanation for awareness levels being low is attributed, to associate in nursing extent, to the frequency of activity fraud risk assessment. One-third of the respondents to the survey don't perform fraud risk assessment because of a perceived lack valuable. This trend is exposing additional organizations to the chance of fraud. As a result, they've probably gapped themselves up to attacks from criminals anyplace within the world. Against a backcloth of information losses and thieving, laptop viruses and hacking, this survey appearance at the importance and impact of this new variety of economic crime and the way it affects businesses worldwide. Cybercrime ranks together of the highest four varieties of economic crime. over 0.5 (58%) understand the info Technology department as a high-risk department with reference to committing cybercrime. ninety-six aforementioned that their organizations monitor internal and external electronic traffic and web-based activity. concerning eightieth of Indian respondents reportable that cybercrime threat originates among India or through a mixture of in and out of doors the country. concerning 2/3rd of respondents failed to have access to rhetorical technology tools that area unit helpful in combating cybercrime. thirty-fifth of respondents failed to have any cybersecurity coaching within the last twelve months. quality misappropriation has not solely been the foremost common variety of economic crime however additionally shown an interesting increase - 2 hundredths in 2007 to sixty-eight in 2011. The nearly simple fraction of the respondents found that the perpetrators were among their own employees. In most cases, perpetrators of fraud were male, between the ages of thirty-one and forty, and educated to degree level or higher. Eightieth respondents aforementioned their organization terminated the individual United Nations agency committed the fraud and over half the respondents ceased to conduct business with outsiders United Nations agency engaged in the fallacious conduct. Despite the growing confidence that organizations surveyed have in their risk management systems most fraud (35 %) remains detected unintentionally.

The cybercrime offers low risks and high rewards as compared to ancient crimes. For instance, in associate in nursing outwardly perpetrated cybercrime, a fraudster infiltrates a banking industry, remotely, to steal cash or personal info. The fraudster is at a lesser risk compared to somebody United Nations agency physically steals assets from a company. There unit fewer risks once committing cybercrime. The fraudster isn't gifted at the location; thence the probabilities of obtaining caught area unit-less. It's tough for enforcement agencies to follow ancient investigatory steps to prosecute the culprit as a result of the various location and jurisdiction of the culprit. The perpetrators will come to the scene of the crime with the comparatively nominal worry of detection.

The money law-breaking includes cheating, MasterCard frauds, money laundering, forgery, on-line investment frauds etc. such crimes area unit punishable underneath each IPC and IT Act. A number one Bank in India was cheated to the extent of 1.39 crores because of misappropriation of funds by manipulation of laptop records relating to debit and credit accounts. Most cases involving a computer-connected fraud are prosecuted underneath existing criminal legislation and this has been adequate to address these offenses. But applying ancient criminal ideas to acts involving intangible info have meant that some amendments have proven necessary to resolve the problems of applying existing definitions to the new technology.

Their area unit varied legislation in India that deals with the Fraud and connected activities, a number of them are: Section twenty-five of Indian legal code will arrange to outline the word fraudulently by an expression that there is no fraud unless there's associate in nursing intention to mulct. In general, fraud is employed in several ways in which viz.

• To deprive a person of his right either by getting one thing by deception or by taking one thing de jure while not the data or consent of the owner.

• To withhold de jure from another, what is due to his or to de jure forestall one from getting what he could just claim.

• To defeat or frustrate de jure another's right to property.

• Whenever the words fraud, intent to mulct or Associate in Nursing intent to reveal some person to actual or attainable injury.

• The most intent and object of the fallacious person is in each case, his own advantage.

A conclusive take a look at on the fallacious character of a deception for criminal functions is whether or not there to is that the deceit derived any advantage from it that he wouldn't have had if the reality has been proverbial. If so, that advantage would typically have a similar in less or risk of less to some other person and if thus, there is fraud. Fraud encompasses among its fold the scam of the net. Each the essential requisites of fraud i.e. deceit or intention to deceive and actually an attainable injury to a private or a gaggle of people area unit gift in such scams. All such scams no matter their procedure, area unit supposed to achieve an advantage for a few nearly always at the chance of loss to others.

Sections 415 to 420, IPC detail the law about cheating, within the case of web Scams relevant sections about the crime of cheating like cheating by impersonation (Section 416) cheating with data that a wrongful loss could guarantee to a person wherever interest if the wrongdoer is absolute to defend (Section 418), etc. is also applied per the facts of the case. The word Fraud is clearly outlined underneath the Indian Contract Act, 1872.

Section seven - "Fraud" Defined: "Fraud" suggests that and includes any of the subsequent acts committed by a celebration to a contractor along with his connivance The IT Act, 2000 deals with the crimes regarding web fraud and online investment fraud in sections 43(d), 65 and 66. Section 43(d) penalizes someone UN agency harms or causes damage to knowledge. 'Damage', below clause (iv) of the clarification, suggests that to destroy, alter, add, modify or arrange any laptop resource by any suggests that. Therefore, unauthorized alteration of information would come back inside the range of section forty-three (d) that is spare to hide laptop crimes like the issue of false stocks or market manipulation schemes since they primarily involve alteration and/or addition of information. Section 65of the IT Act makes meddling with laptop ASCII text file AN offense. 'Computer supply code' has been outlined because of the listing of programmes, laptop commands, style and layout and programme analysis of laptop resource in any type. web fraud would conjointly come back inside the scope of section sixty-six of the IT Act handling wrongful loss or harm to the general public or any individual because of destruction or alteration of any knowledge residing in an exceeding laptop resource or because of decreasing its worth or utility or poignant it injuriously by any suggests that. Alternative connected enactments area unit the businesses Act, 2013 and also the Securities and Exchange Board of India Act, 1992 as conjointly sections 415 to 424 of the IPC referring to cheating.

Cyber Crime associated with Property Rights;

Name violations and spending off

A domain name identifies a pc or a sub Network of computers within the web. In straightforward terms, a site name could be a name-cum-address on the web, of any individual or entity. A pc or device that 'hooked up to the web has associate address popularly called name. With the advancement of web communication and growing e-commerce and its future potential, domain names these days square measure serving as trade names or brands and carry with them the goodwill and name of the websites they represent. Domain names getting used as business identifiers have earned importance and legal holiness as suggests that of differentiation between e-players since e-commerce is conducted in the absence of private interaction or the chance to examine the products.

In Cardservice international Iraqi National Congress. V. Mc Gee, it absolutely was a control that the. it absolutely was an additional control that a site name is quite a mere web address for it additionally identifies the website to people who reach it, very similar to a person's name identifies a specific person. The word 'domain' as per Chambers twenty-first Century lexicon suggests that a territory owned or dominated by one person or Government.

Webster's defines it in numerous contexts as under:—

• A field of action thought, influence;

• Territory ruled by one rule or Government;

• A region characterized by particular features;

• Law;

• Land to that their superior title and absolute possession.

Thus, in common formulation any title or name or mark or complete or identity in any field of activity or a brand over that a specific individual has the exclusive, previous and lone claim is that the name or brand for any reasonable activity. Trademark is at par with a territory and also the owner of any trademark is placed within the same position as owner of the territory. Domain name registrations and protection of a trademark in relation to it have been recognized by courts.

The law concerning passing off is fairly well settled. The principle underlying the action is that no man is entitled to hold on his business in such some way on the result in the assumption that he's carrying on the business of another man or to steer to believe that he's carrying on or has any reference to the business carried on by another man. The principles of common law governing actions of passing off. As control by courts, the aim of this wrongful conduct is to guard industrial goodwill to confirm that people's business reputations aren't exploited. It's supported policy, the necessity to encourage enterprise and to confirm industrial stability.

There is a distinction between legislation concerning logos and also the passing off action; for, whereas registration of relevant mark itself provides title to the registered owner, the burden during a passing off action lies upon the litigant to determine the existence of the business name that he seeks to shield. The quality protected is that the name the plaintiffs business has got to the relevant mark. It's not perpetually necessary that there should be the alive product of that alternative man with that the litigant seeks to confuse his own. Passing off might occur in cases wherever the plaintiffs don't in truth trot out the offending goods.

With the advancement and progress in technology, services rendered within the net has conjointly returned to be recognized and accepted and square measure being given shielding therefore as to protect such supplier of service from passing off the services rendered by others. In an online service, a selected website can be reached by anyone anyplace in the world WHO proposes to go to the aforementioned website. As a matter of reality during a matter wherever services rendered through the name within the net, a really alert vigil is critical and a strict read is to be taken for its easy accessibility and reach by anyone from any corner of the world. it's conjointly determined that considering the sizeableness of the net and its comparatively recent availableness to the general public, several net users aren't refined enough to tell apart between the refined distinction within the domain names of the parties.

The degree of the similarity of the marks sometimes is vitally necessary Associate in nursing vital in an action for passing off. There's each risk of an online user being incoherent and deceived in a basic cognitive process that both the domain names belong to one common supply and association, though the 2 belong to 2completely different considerations. As command by the Supreme Court, the word 'India' extra to 1 mark is of no consequence. So there's each risk of the net users to believe that 'Yahoo India' is another name in the series of Yahoo marks/ names and thereby there is each risk of confusion being created and thereby preventing these users from reaching the net website of a litigant, 'Yahoo.com'. In another case, the defendants were found producing, selling or offering purchasable the merchandise like Supari and chew Tobacco below the trademark 'Yahoo'.

Under the trademark INFOSYS, the litigant company was incorporated within the year 1981 and has attained a really high degree of goodwill having nonheritable the standing of one of the leading exporters of pc code. Defendants use of trademark/ name INFOSYS, conjointly engaged in manufacturing business, amounts to infringement of the plaintiffs registered trademark numbers. Defendants hosted a web siteweb.blitzerinfosys.com and mark INFOSYS was denote on such website conspicuously.

Pen Books Pvt. Ltd. got registered the name 'penbooks.com' in 1999 however, thanks to some technical snags couldn't launch the website. The validity amount of registration of the aforementioned name invalid on 2-3-2001. Once the litigant wanted to launch the website once more in 2002, it found that the name 'penbooks.com' stood registered within the name of the litigant and it had been publicized on the net purchasable. The Court found such a registration within the name of the litigant to be associate in the nursing abusive registration of domain name in violation of the rights of logos and repair marks. Considering the Uniform name Disputes Resolution Policy, the Court found that the domain name having been registered by the litigant for the purpose of selling or transferring an equivalent was to be treated as having been registered in dangerous religion.

Code Piracy

Copyright subsists throughout Asian country within the following categories of works:-

• Original literary, dramatic and musical;

• Inventive works;

• PC Programme;

• Cinematograph films; and

• Audio recording.

Microsoft Corporation, an organization world famed for its business code like Microsoft Windows, Microsoft workplace etc. that square measure put in and used on millions of computers everywhere the planet, together with an Asian country, conjointly manufacturer an outsized vary of pc peripherals (hardware). The corporate received info that the defendants square measure infringing their copyright by carrying on the business of unauthorized hard disc loaded i.e. pre-loading numerous software's of the litigant company onto the fixed disk of the pc that was being assembled and sold by them. The code loaded onto the machine, naturally, weren't in the midst of the initial Media, being the CD (s) / Floppy Discs, Certificates of genuineness (COA), user licence Agreements (EULAs), User Instruction Manuals, Registration Cards then thereon accompany the plaintiff's real code. The litigant, in spite of notice, had did not respond. The Court command it as a willful, intentional and crying violation by the litigant of plaintiff's copyrights in MS-DOS and trademark in Microsoft.

Section 43(b) of the data Technology Act, 2000 provides compensation and imposes a liability to pay damages by method of compensation if any individual while not permission downloads, copies or extracts any knowledge; pc database or info from such pc, computer knowledge processing system ADP or network together with info or data commander hold on in any removable medium. Section forty-three covers 2 problems concerning 'Data Protection and Privacy' i.e. Unauthorised access to automatic data processing system and unauthorized downloading/copying of knowledge.

Communication

The use of data technology by terrorist organizations isn't restricted to running websites and analysis in databases. Within the context of the investigations once the 9/11 attacks, it had been reported that the terrorists used e-mail communication for coordination of their attacks. The press reported on the exchange via e-mail of careful directions regarding the targets and therefore the range of attackers. By victimization encoding technology and suggests that of anonymous communication, the human activity parties will create it even harder to spot and monitor terrorist communication.

Cyber Terrorist Act

Cyber-terrorist act is a sexy choice for contemporary terrorists for many reasons.

• It's cheaper than ancient terrorist ways.

• Cyber-terrorist act is a lot of anonymous than ancient terrorist ways.
.

• The variability and range of targets are huge.

• Cyber-terrorist act may be conducted remotely, a feature that's particularly appealing to terrorists.

• Cyber-terrorist act has the potential to have an effect on directly a bigger range of individuals.

The terrorist act development is an incredibly advanced issue within the current generation. The attacks of terrorist on the man have inflated speedily in last decade. Everybody from traditional individuals to the statehood of the country has suffered thanks to the violent act of terrorist activity. The threat of terrorism has become a challenge for the globe once post-conflict. The state agencies aren't adequate enough to tackle or management the surprise attack on humankind; numbers of individuals were killed by the inhuman act of the terrorists worldwide. Many countermeasures area unit adopted by the national and international front however they were did not manage the surprise attack. However, most of those are unit designed in a very typical pattern, which could achieve success in very usual terror attacks. However, at this time, we tend to sleep in digital age and computers and we also are enjoying in their part and becomes a great tool within the hands of a terrorist.

A number of economies were thrown into disarray with the recent money turmoil. Opinions stay divided on that method the road ahead results in. however even once home names and trade heavyweights were being brought down to their knees, technology remained steadfast. In fact, technology these days has therefore inconspicuously become a business enabler that it's nearly simple to overlook. A replacement page within the war book comes in a very sinister kind. Cyber-terrorism of terrorist act terrorist act involves extremely targeted efforts created with the intention of terrorism. Disassociate rising threat that has the potential to cause serious harm. Whereas we'd typically associate the terrorist act with loss of life, we tend to cannot overlook necessary results like intimidation or coercion that may be led to by cyberwar. A prolonged and targeted terrorist act campaign against a rustic has the potential to render it weak within the semi-permanent. Given the various economic, financial, and even psychological effects such a campaign may have, cyber-terrorist act poses an important hurdle in times to come back. Technology is the backbone of most countries in the world these days. A tough hit on such an essential backbone would be a perfect strategy for attackers. The UN telecommunications agency warns that consecutive war may somewhat be in Net. This could come back as no surprise. Wars have typically enclosed attacks on installations or facilities that area unit essential to the enemy, delivering an incapacitating blow to realize the upper ground. Considering the sheer magnitude of dependence that the trendy world places on technology, it might logically build a fine target if a war were to turn up.

Cyber-terrorist act becomes an associate international threat to the international population as through the terrorist act, the terrorist area unit spreading false info in line with political and non-secular ideologies. The word "Cyber Terrorism" is of recent vintage and was coined by pc whiz Barry C. Collin. The Term cyber terrorism is that the combination of Net and terrorism and that we don't have any definition of cyber terrorism which might be accepted worldwide. Each investigator or scholar in the subject offers a unique dimension whereas shaping the term cyber terrorist act. During this analysis, the definition of the cyber-terrorist act is split into intent primarily based and impact based. It refers to attacks on the computers, networks and network grids of the country that heavily depend upon networks and make disturbance or concern among the minds of its voters.

Definition of Cyber terrorist act

The definition of the cyber-terrorist act cannot be created intensive because the nature of the crime is such it should be left to be comprehensive in nature. The character of "cyberspace" is such a new mode and tools area unit fictional regularly; therefore it's not informed place the definition in a very garment formula or pigeons hole. In fact, the primary effort of the judiciary ought to be to know the definition as munificently to penalize the terrorist strictly, therefore the government will tackle the evil of the cyber-terrorist act.

Some efforts are created to outline cyber terrorist act exactly. Most notably, Dorothy Denning, a academic computing, has an advocate associate commendable unambiguous definition before the House Armed Services Committee in could 2000: "Cyber terrorism act of terrorist is that the convergence of Net and terrorism. It refers to unlawful attacks and threats of attacks against computers, networks and therefore the data hold on in this once done to intimidate or have a government or its individuals in furtherance of political or social objectives. Attacks that cause death or bodily injury, explosions or severe economic loss would be examples. Serious attacks against essential infrastructures may be acts of the cyber-terrorist act, betting on their impact. Attacks that disrupt nonessential services or that area unit primarily a pricey nuisance wouldn't."

According to the North Atlantic Treaty Organization (2008), cyber-terrorist act is "a cyber-attack exploitation or exploiting pc or communication networks to cause ample destruction to generate concern or intimidate a society into the associate ideologic goal."

In the Federal Government, the Federal Bureau of Investigation describes the cyber-terrorist act as:

"Cyber-terrorism may be a criminal act perpetrated by the utilization of computers and telecommunications capabilities, leading to violence, destruction and/or disruption of services to for concern by inflicting confusion and uncertainty among a given population, with the goal of influencing a government or population to evolve to a selected political, social, or philosophic agenda". A universal acknowledged definition of the cyber-terrorist act is "a criminal.

The U.S. Federal Bureau of Investigation defines a cyber-terrorist act as "Cyber terrorist act is any plotted, politically motivated attack against data, laptop systems, laptop programs, and information which ends in violence against non-combatant targets by sub-national teams or hugger-mugger agents."

The Former chief strategian at Netscape, Kevin Coleman, has given the definition of cyber-terrorist act as: "The plotted use of troubled activities, or the threat the refrom, against computers and/or networks, with the intention to cause hurt or more social, philosophic, religious, political or similar objectives or to intimidate somebody in furtherance of such objectives."

The term cybercrime and cyber-terrorist act are totally different all at once we have a tendency to can't say that each cybercrime is a cyber-terrorist act. We've got to ascertain whether or not the cybercrime is politically and ideologically motivated or not, to tag it as cyber-terrorist act. In gift situation, the aim of the foreign terrorist organization is to destroy the communication, infrastructure, transportation and money network of the country through the utilization of computers and networks to form concern within the minds of the folks, as each country within the world is heavily reliant upon the technology. Recent attacks in Asian country furthermore as in world have proven that the terrorist also is utilizing the computers and networking to carry out terrorist attacks.

Objectives of the Cyber terrorist act

The Basic objective of the cyber foreign terrorist organization whereas assaultive a nation, an area and a company, to destroy tangible property or assets and killing kith and kin to prove their agenda or political ideologies, therefore there's little question that technology advancement in computers and networking has vied an important half in providing them chance, that influenced terrorist ways and behavior significantly.

3 major objectives in cyber terrorism

1. Following the intelligence reports, terrorist teams these days recourse to the net on a daily basis. Their data and skills in relevancy technology are steadily growing and this build-up of information and skills would eventually offer the mandatory experience for locating

and exploiting vulnerabilities within the online security systems of governments or vital infrastructure establishments. Although those researching the terrorist use of the web usually. Furthermore, the structure perform of cyber-terrorist act allows the wrongdoers to pursue their objective either through the suggests that of ancient warfare or technology.

2. The ways used are defacing, denying, and exposing. Since the Western countries are extremely obsessed with on-line structures supporting important services, these ways are of well-tried advantage. However, troubled activities typically don't entail grave consequences, except maybe in cases of the haphazard upshot.

3. This purpose is directed towards achieving the same or similar results as a classical terrorist act, it's labeled pure cyber terrorist act. Through the utilization of technology and therefore the web, the terrorists get to visit destruction or injury on tangible property or assets and even death or injury to people. There aren't any cases of pure cyber terrorist act up to this point, however, maybe its incidence is just a matter of your time, given the actual fact that the states' vital infrastructures have important security flaws.

Whether or not the Threat is real or not

The danger caused by cyber-terrorist act has grabbed the eye of the mass media, the safety community, IT industries, Defence sector, politicians, and specialises in form of fields have popularized a situation during which cyber terrorists electronically forced an entry computers that management dams or traffic management systems, wreaking disturbance and endangering not solely voluminous lives but national security itself.

Just, however, the reality is that the threat that cyber coercion poses? As a result of most important infrastructure in today's world is networked through computers, the potential threat from cyber coercion is extremely minatory. Cyber-terrorist through the assistance of Hackers will gain access to sensitive info and to the operation of crucial services and may cripple or a minimum of disabling the military, financial, and repair sectors of advanced economies.

The growing reliance of our societies on computers and web has created a replacement sort of vulnerability, giving terrorists the possibility to approach targets that might rather be totally watertight, like national defense systems and traffic management systems. A lot of technologically developed a rustic is a lot of vulnerable it becomes to cyber attacks against its infrastructure. Concern concerning the potential danger expose by cyber coercion is therefore well supported. The Crime associated with the Internet has been increasing rapidly; but there is no cyber terrorist act in Indian public facilities, transport systems, atomic power plants, power grids, or different key machinery of the national infrastructure. Cyber attacks area unit regular, however they need not been distributed by terrorists and that they haven't wanted to communicate the sort of injury that might qualify them as cyber coercion.

Recent Incident of Cyber coercion in World

The following area unit the quantity of incident that has created issues for nations or which might be termed as a terrorist act by the FTO with the assistance of knowledge technology within the world – Cyber Attacks in the geographical region With the center, East Conflict at an awfully heated moment between bordering countries Pro-Palestinian associated Pro-Israel Cyber teams are launching an offensive against websites and mail services utilized by the political sectors the opposing teams show support for. The attacks had been reported by the NIPC (National Infrastructure Protection Center) in Oct of 2000 to U.S. Officials.

Terrorist Funding

Most terrorist organizations depend upon monetary resources they receive from third parties. Tracing back these monetary transactions has become one among the key approaches within the fight against coercion once the 9/11 attacks. One among the most difficulties during this respect is that the incontrovertible fact that the monetary resources needed to hold out attacks don't seem to be essentially passive. There unit many ways in which within which web services may be used for terrorist funding. Terrorist organizations will create use of electronic payment systems to modify on-line donations. They'll use websites to publish info a way to gift, e.g. that checking account ought to be used for transactions. Associate degree example of such associate degree approach is the organization "Hizb al-Tahrir", that printed bank-account info for potential donors. Another approach is that the implementation of online credit-card donations. Irish Republican Army (IRA) was one of the primary terrorist organizations that collected donations via MasterCard. Each approach carries the chance that the printed info is discovered and wont to trace back monetary transactions. It's so possible that anonymous electronic payment systems can become additional standard. To avoid discovery, terrorist organizations are attempting to cover their activities by involving non-suspicious players like charity organizations. Another (Internet-related) approach is that the operation of faux web shops. It's comparatively easy to line up a web search on the net. One among the largest benefits of the network is that the incontrovertible fact that businesses may be operated worldwide. Proving that monetary transactions that befell on those sites don't seem to be regular purchases however donations aren't in the least simple. It might be necessary to research each dealings – which may be troublesome if the net search is operated in an exceedingly completely different jurisdiction or anonymous payment systems area unit used.

Attacks against essential infrastructures

In addition to regular pc crimes like fraud and fraud, attacks against essential info infrastructures might become a goal for terrorists. The growing reliance on info technology makes essential infrastructure additional liable to attacks. This is often particularly the case with relevancy attacks against interconnected systems that area unit connected by pc and communication networks. In those cases, the disruption caused by a network-based attack goes on the far side the failure of one system. Even short interruptions to services might cause large monetary injury to e-commerce businesses – not just for civil services however additionally for military infrastructure and services. Investigation or perhaps preventing such attacks presents distinctive challenges. In contrast to physical attacks, the offenders don't get to be a gift at the place wherever the impact of the attack happens. And whereas effecting the attack the offenders will use suggests that of anonymous communication and encoding technology to conceal their identity.

Critical infrastructure is well known as a possible target for terrorist attacks because it is by definition important for a state's property and stability. Associate degree infrastructure is taken into account to be essential if its incapacity or destruction would have a weakening impact on the defense or economic security of a state. This area unit in particular: power systems, telecommunication systems, gas and oil storage and transportation, banking and finance, transportation, facility systems and emergency services. The degree of civil disturbance caused by the disruption of services by cyclone Katrina in

U.S. highlights the dependence of society on the convenience of those services. The malicious software system "Stuxnet" underlines the rising threat expose by Internet-based attacks that specialize in essential infrastructure. In 2010, a security firm in the Republic of Belarus discovered a brand new malicious software system. Analysis into the manipulations caused by the software system, the designer and therefore the motivation continues to be in progress and far and away not all the facts are discovered, particularly in relevancy attribution and motivation of the designer.

However, particularly with relevancy the functioning of the software system, there appears to be a rather solid reality basis by now:

The advanced software system, with additional than 4000 functions, was reported to target industrial management systems (ICS)– specifically those created by the technology company Siemens. It had been distributed through removable drives and used four zero-day exploits for the infection of pc systems. Infected pc systems have principally been reported from Islamic Republic of Iran, Dutch East Indies and the Islamic Republic of Pakistan, however additionally from the North American country and European countries. Though the malicious software system is usually characterized as extremely subtle, their area unit reports that question the degree of sophistication.

As indicated higher than, the determination of attribution and motive is harder and still extremely unsure. News reports and studies speculate that the software system might have targeted the metal enrichment facilities in the Islamic Republic of Iran and caused a delay within the country's nuclear programme.

Two main conclusions may be drawn from the invention of the malicious software system. 1st of all, the incident underlines that essential infrastructure is basically addicted to technology and attacks area unit potential. Secondly, the very fact that the software system was distributed among different ways, through removable drives highlights that merely disconnecting pc systems from the net doesn't forestall attacks.

The dependence of essential infrastructure on ICT goes on the far side the energy and nuclear trade. This may be incontestable by lightness of a number of incidents associated with transportation, that is in most countries additionally thought of a part of the essential infrastructure. One potential target of associate degree attack is that the arrival system. The arrival systems of most airports within the world area unit already supported interconnected pc systems. In 2004, the Sasser pc worm infected a lot of computers around the world, among them pc systems of major airlines, that forced, the cancellation of flights.

Another potential target is online ticketing systems. Today, a major range of tickets area unit purchased online. Airlines use info technology for numerous operations. All major airlines permit their customers to shop for tickets online. Like different e-commerce activities, those online services may be targeted by offenders. One common technique wont to attack web-based services is denial-of-service (DOS) attacks. In 2000, at intervals a brief time, many DOS attacks were launched against well-known corporations like CNN, e-Bay, and Amazon. As a result, a number of the services weren't accessible for many hours or perhaps days. Airlines are stricken by DOS attacks moreover. In 2001 the Lufthansa website was the target of associate degree attack.

Finally, an extra potential target for Internet-related attacks against essential transportation infrastructure is the landing field management system. The vulnerability of computer-controlled flight management systems was incontestable by a hacking attack against Worcester landing field within the North American country in 1997.

Throughout the hacking attack, the bad person disabled phone services to the landing field tower and finish off the system managing the runway lights.

Breach of Privacy and Confidentiality

Privacy refers to the proper of Associate in nursing individual/s to see once, however and to what extent his or her personal information is shared with others. Breach of privacy means that unauthorized use or distribution or revelation of private data. Confidentiality means that non-disclosure of data to unauthorized or unwanted persons. Additionally, to private data some alternative another style of data that helpful for business and outflow of such data to other persons could cause harm to business or person, such data ought to be protected.

Generally for protective secrecy of such data, parties whereas sharing information forms associate in nursing agreement regarding the procedure of handling of data knowledge and to not disclose such data to 3rd parties or use it in such the simplest way that it'll be disclosed to 3rd parties. Persistently party or their workers leak such valuable data for warning gains and causes a breach of contract of confidentiality. Special techniques like Social Engineering square measure usually won't to acquire direction.

Copyright crimes

The switch from analog to digital distribution of copyright-protected content marks a turning purpose in copyright violation. The copy of music design and videos has traditionally been restricted since the copy of associate degree analog supply was typically in the middle of a loss of quality of the copy, that successively limits the choice to use the copy as a supply for more reproductions. With the switch to digital sources, quality is preserved and consistent quality copies became potential.

The showbiz has responded by implementing technical measures (digital rights management or DRM) to stop copy, however heretofore these measures have usually been circumvented shortly when their introduction. Varied computer code tools are out there over the net that alters users to repeat music CDs and motion-picture show DVDs protected by DRM-systems. Additionally, the net offers unlimited distribution opportunities. As a result, the infringement of holding rights (especially of copyright) may be a wide committed offense over the net.

Copyright and Digital Music

The fast Increase of the net has created it potential to transfer large knowledge of all sorts over the net in a very easy and price effective approach. More compression technology has conjointly contended important role in transferring knowledge at the quick speed and in less time. In A& M Records opposition. v. Napster opposition. Conjointly referred to as Napster's case is considered to be the landmark 1st case wherever lawfulness of digital music sharing over the net was questioned. Napster, on the net, had modified the approach individuals hear the music. Individuals may transfer free package from defendant's website and this package lets them share music within the sort ofMP3 files. Essentially Napster developed a package known as Napster's Music Share package, that is on the market freed from the charge from Napster's site, and Napster's network server. It expedited the transmission of MP3 files between and among its users, through peer-to-peer (P2P) file sharing, Napster allowed its users to:

(1) Store MP3 music files on individual pc laborious drives obtainable for copyright by alternative Napster users;

(2) Rummage around for MP3 music files held on alternative users' computers;

(3) Transfer actual copies of the contents of alternative users' MP3 files from one pc to a different via the net.

Napster became the fashion among music fans notably in faculties and universities around the USA. the employment of Napster's website was thus high that many faculties had to ban it from their networks, not as a result of it had been banned however as a result of its significant usage was taking on monumental amounts of information measure. For the young company, there may hardly be any higher news.

There was only 1 very little downside. Recording corporations that turn out the music within the 1st place have copyrights on them and what Napster started doing was questionable and banned. it's not that Napster was unaware of the potential legal downside however it had been hoping its new technology would let it survive within the court by employing a "fair use" defense against infringement of copyright charges since no one oversubscribed the music to anyone else however simply distributed it for complimentary. Therefore, Napster hoped to strike a trot out the recording corporations and really work with them instead of fight with them.

However, this didn't happen. The Recording business Association of America (RIM) sued Napster for copyright violation. A grievance was filed against Napster for an injunction as he was a contributive and vicarious copyright infringer.

Napster raised 'fair use' defense which has uses for such functions as criticism, comment, news reportage, teaching (including multiple copies for the classroom), scholarship, or analysis. It's vital to notice that if a user is truthful then it's not an infringement of copyright. It knew 3 specific uses in practice:

1. Sampling, wherever users build temporary copies of a piece before purchasing;

2. space-shifting, wherever users access an audio recording through the Napster system that they already own in audio compact disc format; and

3. Permissive distribution of recordings by each new and established artists.

The Court applied the subsequent factors to determine whether or not truthful philosophy is applied:

1. The aim and character of the use;

2. The character of proprietary work;

3. The quantity and materiality of the portion utilized in respect to the work as a whole; and

4. The result of the employment upon the potential marketplace for the work or the worth of the work.

The court command that Napster users aren't truthful users because:

1. Downloading MP3 files doesn't remodel the proprietary work;

2. Proprietary musical compositions and sound recordings area unit artistic in nature and so would like copyright protection;

3. Users interact in the wholesale repetition of proprietary work as a result of files transfer essentially involves repetition of the completeness of the proprietary work;

4. Harms the market in a minimum of 2 ways: it reduces audio compact disc sales among faculty students and it raises barriers to plaintiff's entry into the marketplace for the digital downloading of music.

On July 26,2000, the District Court for the Northern District of CA granted plaintiffs a preliminary injunction, so prevented litigant Napster from participating in, or facilitating, or distributing plaintiff's proprietary musical compositions and sound recordings, while not categorical permission of the proper house owners.

The Court command that a majority of Napster users use the service to transfer and transfer proprietary music and by doing that, it constitutes direct infringement of plaintiff's musical compositions, recordings. Concerning contributive infringement of copyright, the Court command that: the record clearly shows that Napster had true information that specific infringing material was obtainable exploitation its system. That it may block access to the infringing material and however it didn't take away the fabric.

Therefore, it's responsible for the infringement of copyright. More the District The court, by an order, obligatory an obligation: on the company to inform Napster of specific infringing files; and on Napster to perpetually search its index and block all such explicit files. The record corporations appealed, however, this order was upheld and it had been reaffirmed that the plaintiffs were purported to give notice to Napster of its proprietary music files before Napster was to forestall access to such objectionable content. Meaning that Napster still must take away proprietary material whenever it had been created responsive to its presence on its network. As Napster was unable to try to this thus, it had been left with no choice, however, to close up its service in Gregorian calendar month 2001.

Rights of copy and info

Info could be an assortment of information in a computer network, that is organized in order that its contents will simply be accessed, managed and updated. It's vital to notice that copyrights are equally affected if a copyright material of the author is reproduced in an electronic kind while not his consent and created a part of a info. In big apple Times Co. v. Tasini, there was an agreement between six freelance authors and publishers whereby the articles of authors were to be revealed in 3 print periodicals. However, while not the freelancer's consent, 2 on-line database firms placed copies of the freelancers' articles, at the side of all different articles from the periodicals during which the freelancers' work appeared, into 3 databases. The freelance authors' grievance alleged that their copyrights had been infringed by the inclusion of their articles within the databases. The publishers, in response, relied on the privilege of copy and distribution accorded them by Section 201(c) of Digital Millennium Copyright Act, 1998.

The US Supreme Court control that the Electronic Publishers infringed the author's copyrights by reproducing and distributing the articles in a way not approved by the authors and not privileged by Section 201(c). It was more control that even the Print Publishers infringed the authors' copyrights by authorizing the Electronic Publishers to position the articles within the Databases and by aiding the Electronic Publishers in this endeavor.

In Kelly v. Arriba Soft house., the litigator, Leslie Kelly, an expert artist had proprietary several of his pictures of the yank West. A number of these pictures were settled on Kelly's website or on different websites with that Kelly had a license agreement. The suspect, Arriba Soft Corporation operated an online program that displayed its ends up in the shape of tiny footage instead of a lot of usual sort of text. Arriba maintained its info of pictures of pictures by repetition images from different websites together with the plaintiff's website. By clicking on one among this tiny footage, referred to as thumbnails, the user may read an oversized version of that very same image among the context of the Arriba website.

Subsequently, litigator, Kelly discovered that his pictures were a part of Arriba's program info, he filed a suit for violation. The District Court found that plaintiff; Kelly had established a clear case of violation supported Arriba's unauthorized copy and show of Kelly's works, however that this copy and show deep-rooted a non-infringing enjoyment below Section 107 of the Digital Millennium Copyright Act 1998. Kelly filed a charm within the Circuit Court that control that "the creation and also the use of the thumbnails within the program could be an enjoyment, however the show of the larger image could be a violation of Kelly's prerogative to publically show his works. This use of Kelly's image doesn't quantity to repetition them, however, rather, mercantilism them directly from Kelly's website. Therefore it can't be a violation supported copy of proprietary works. Instead, this use of Kelly's image infringes upon Kelly's prerogative to show the proprietary work publically.

Software package Piracy

Software piracy refers to the dirty repetition of real programs or the counterfeiting and distribution of merchandise supposed to pass for the first. These reasonable crimes additionally embody violation, emblems violations, larceny of laptop ASCII text file, patent violations etc. Domain names square measure additionally emblems and protected by ICANN domain dispute resolution policy and additionally underneath trademark laws. Cyber squatters register name clone of well-liked service supplier name therefore on attract their users and obtain get pleasure from them.

India and Asian country Conflict

As tensions between the neighbor regions of India and Asian country over Cashmere grew over time, Pro-Pakistan cyber-terrorists and recruited hackers began to focus on India's web Community. Simply before and once the Gregorian calendar month eleventh attacks, it's believed that the sympathizers of Asian country began their unfold of information and attacks against Indian web based mostly communities. teams like and Doctor Nuker have marred or non-continuous service to many major entities in India such as the Z TV Network, The India Institute of Science and therefore the Bhabha Atomic center that all have political ties. The Group, Pakistani Hackerz Club conjointly went as so much on target us Air Force Computing atmosphere and therefore the Department of Energy's website.

Retribution by China

In could 1999 the accidental bombing of a Chinese embassy in Serbia and Montenegro by U.S. Bombers, junction rectifier to a colossal website disfigurement and email bombardment attack on Yankee corporations and agencies. Professional Chinese hackers and political teams dead the attacks to realize empathy for Chinese cause. Federal government sites like the North American nation department of energy and therefore the interior and therefore the parkland Service were all hit and had website marred along with the White House website. The sites were cut down for 3 days by continual e-mail bombing. Though the attack was rather random and temporary and affected a little range of U.S. sites, the results may are worse.

Yugoslavia Conflict

When international organization air strikes hit Former Republic of Serbia and Montenegro in Kosovo and Serbia, international organization internet servers were subjected to sustained attacks by hackers utilized by the Yugoslav military. All NATO's a hundred servers were subjected to "ping saturation", Distributed Denial Of service assaults and bombarded with thousands of e-mails, several containing viruses.

Communications infrastructures

Cyber Attack on Esthonia

The small Baltic country of Esthonia was cyber-attacked from Russia. Ever since the govt. of the geographical region determined to get rid of a war memorial to the Red Army from an sq. within the capital, Tallinn, Russian outrage has ensued. This took the shape of demonstrations and even riots. Then again one thing extraordinary happened: quickly, and completely swiftly, the total country was subjected to a barrage of cyber-warfare, disabling the websites of state ministries, political parties, banks, and newspapers. Techniques ordinarily utilized by cybercriminals, like vast remotely- controlled networks of hijacked computers, were accustomed to cripple very important public services. The international organization has sent its prime terrorism consultants to Tallinn, with western democracies caught on the hop over the implications of such associate track. The Estonian defense ministry said: "We've been lucky to survive this. If associate flying field, bank or state infrastructure is attacked by a missile, it's clear war however if an equivalent result's done by computer's, then what does one decision It. IS It a state of war? These queries should be addressed ." Esthonia has curst Russia, predictably enough; that, if true, would mean this is often the primary cyber attack by one sovereign state upon another. The Estonian attacks were a lot of seemingly to be the work of angry young Russian hackers operating alone than any type of union blitz by the Kremlin. However either manner, the implications area unit serious.

Sony PlayStation Network, Microsoft's Xbox Live network case

In this case, the confidential knowledge of the workers and their families has been leaked in 2014. The corporate has featured loss in revenue because of movies being leaked, sensitive worker data was disclosed as well as their salaries and social insurance numbers, and Gov. emails were heralded. The attack was hatched by the Lizard Squad, a corporation that refers to itself as a computer programmer. Then they launched a colossal Distributed denial of service attack against Sony's PlayStation Network and Microsoft's Xbox Live networks. They followed up these disruptions with associate attack against the Tor Project, a network of virtual tunnels that enable folks and teams to boost their privacy and security on the web and at the moment Asian nation attacked the network infrastructure and network has gone down for pretty much 10 hours because of the attack poignant the lives of millions. Because of that several suppose that it's associate act by the US Government. But it's not, however, they manage to make doubts concerning getting the merchandise among the patron and folks concerning the transnational corporations. The Motive behind these cyber terrorist attacks is casualty concerned and therefore the obvious ties to geopolitical things that we tend to see in such a large amount of attacks. The present President Barack Obama of us has same that "cyber-terrorist act is probably one amongst the best threats against the U.S. today.

Sadly, the attacks don't seem to be solely here to remain, however, given the utter reliance on the web nowadays, they're seemingly to grow during a very serious manner".

Hacking with ADP system

The title of the same section sixty-six was a name, that created confusion. It had been widely believed as if section sixty-six was the sole legal provision that forbidden the offense of hacking an ADP system. This confusion has been done away with, by bound amendments created by the I.T. (Amendment) Act, 2008. The words "Hacking with pc System" are deleted from section sixty-six, the scope of that has been considerably widened:

"If any individual, deceitfully or fraudulently, will any act spoke in section forty-three, he shall be punishable with imprisonment for a term which can be 3 years or with fine which can be 5100000 rupees or with both".

The various species of the offense of hacking that square measure provided (even though not referred to as 'hacking' specifically) for or might have parts of hacking, within the amended version of the I.T. Act, 2000 are:

• Access to a pc.

• Downloading, repetition or extraction of information from a pc.

• Introducing bug and contaminants.

• Causing harm to a pc.

• Causing disruption of a pc.

146

- Causing denial of access to a pc.

- Affecting vital info infrastructure.

- Cyber coercion.

Council of Europe Convention on crime

The Convention on crime seeks to criminalize associate degree undue manipulation within the course of information process with the intention to impart a hot transfer of property, by providing a piece on the computer- connected fraud:

Article eight – Computer-related fraud

Each Party shall adopt such legislative and alternative measures as is also necessary to ascertain as criminal offenses below its domestic law, once committed by design and while not right, the inflicting of a loss of property to a different person by:

a. any input, alteration, deletion or suppression of laptop knowledge,
b. any interference with the functioning of an ADP system, with dishonorable or dishonest intent of procuring, while not right, associate degree economic profit for oneself or for an additional person.

The acts coated

Article eight a) contains an inventory of the foremost relevant acts of computer-related fraud. "Input" of laptop knowledge covers all reasonably input manipulation like feeding incorrect knowledge into the laptop the PC likewise as computer code manipulations and alternative acts of interference within the course of information process. "Alteration" refers to the modification of existing knowledge. The term "suppression" of laptop knowledge denotes associate degree action that affects the supply of information. "Deletion" corresponds to the definition of the term in Article four covering acts wherever info is removed.

In addition to the list of acts, Article 8, sub-paragraph b) contains the final clause that criminalizes fraud-related "interference with the functioning of a laptop system". The final clause was added to the list of coated acts so as to depart the supply receptive more developments.

The instructive Report points out that "interference with the functioning of a laptop system" covers acts like hardware manipulations, acts suppressing printouts and acts touching recording or flow of information, or the sequence within which programs are run.

Economic loss

Under the most national legal code, the criminal act should end in an associate degree economic loss. The Convention on crime follows an identical idea and limits lawmaking to those acts wherever the manipulations manufacture direct economic or possessory loss of another person's property together with cash, tangibles associate degreed intangibles with a value.

Mental part

As for the opposite offenses listed, Article eight of the Council of Europe Convention on crime needs that the wrongdoer has acted by design. This intent refers to the manipulation likewise because of the loss.

In addition, the Convention on crime needs that the wrongdoer has acted with a dishonorable or dishonest intent to achieve economic or alternative profit for self or alternative. As samples of acts excluded from criminal liability thanks to lack of specific intent, the instructive Report mentions industrial practices arising from market competition that will cause economic hurt to at least one person and profit to a different, however, that don't seem to be disbursed with dishonorable or dishonest intent.

Without right

Computer-related fraud will solely be prosecuted below Article eight of the Convention on crime if it's disbursed "without right". This includes the need that the economic profit should be obtained while not right. The drafters of the Convention on crime discovered that acts disbursed consistent to a legitimate contract between the affected persons don't seem to be thought-about to be while not right. Commonwealth laptop and Computer-related Crimes Model Law the 2002 Commonwealth Model Law will not contain a provision criminalizing computer-related fraud.

Stanford Draft International Convention

The informal 1999 Stanford Draft International Convention doesn't contain a provision criminalizing computer-related fraud.

Misuse of social media and freedom of speech and expression

Indeed, as explained higher than, whereas it is also content on the web that's seen as socially objectionable, abundant of it's not objectionable within the legal sense by any suggests that. However, the determination of whether or not or not a selected set of facts violates the law will solely be created by the judiciary or by the associate freelance body that's freed from political, industrial and different unwarranted influences. Wherever discretionary powers are given to the authorities to form such assessments, this is often only too seemingly to lead to misuse, any contributory to a chilling result that already exists, as India's voters more and more begin to censor themselves.

 The term applies to the depiction of the act instead of the act itself, so doesn't embody live exhibitions like sex shows and striptease. The first subjects of sexy depictions are sexy models, World Health Organization cause for still pictures, and sexy actors or porno stars, World Health Organization perform in pornographic films. If dramatic skills don't seem to be concerned, a performing artist in an exceedingly porno film may additionally be referred to as a model.

Pornography is rampant at intervals of society. It's an endemic that's damaging the lives of tykes, destroying marriages, manufacturing false views of sex and sweetness, and degrading girls. The porno trade has exaggerated speedily, and its exaggerated convenience has weakened ethical and public standards that have historically stood hostile porno. The mix of the weakening ethical normal and therefore the exaggerated convenience has caused its effects to become even a lot of widespread, creating correct teaching regarding porno a necessity. According to Family Safe Media, porno is a $57 billion worldwide trade, as well as $12 billion in us alone the typical email user receives 4.5 sexy emails daily, and therefore the average age of initial exposure to web porno is eleven years previous. Whereas porno is usually solely related to men, a big portion of web porno users are feminine. Family Safe Media reports that seventy-two of web porno viewers are men and twenty-eighth of viewers are feminine.

Laws control the Production, Distribution and Possession of kid porn The UNCRC provides a baseline international legal customary for the protection of youngsters from sexual exploitation. Article 34, among different articles that compel the degrading treatment of youngsters, expressly needs countries to require "all acceptable national, bilateral, and tripartite measures to forestall ... the inducement or coercion of a baby to interact in any unlawful sexuality ... [and] the exploitive use of youngsters in sexy performances and materials." The international organization Commission on Human Rights' Programme of Action for the bar of the Sale of youngsters, kid vice crime and porno reinforces the UNCRC and international efforts to sanction those that exploit kids for sexy functions.

Asia and therefore the Pacific Rim

Article a hundred seventy-five of the Japanese legal code forbids the written portrayal of adult genitalia, intercourse, and crotch hair. However, such illustration of children's genital organ isn't strictly regulated. Moreover, Japanese industrial producers have created ingenious ways to avoid prosecution or enforcement intervention by making sexually specific materials which simply barely avoid depiction of prohibited body elements. Many different Asian nations have recently adopted porno laws. 18 years getting on. The 1993 kid protection law passed within the Philippines (Republic Act No. 7610) includes a provision that prohibits the utilization or coercion of youngsters but eighteen years getting on to perform in obscene exhibitions or indecent shows, whether or not live or video, or to model in an obscene publication or sexy materials. It conjointly imposes sanctions on the sale or distribution of such materials.

Sri Lanka (Penal Code Sec. 286A) passed similar legislation in 1995 that protects kids up to eighteen years getting on. In the Kingdom of Cambodia, a draft proposal (Law on the abolishment of kid Trafficking and vice crime, Art. 9 Ai, ii, iii) for a law against kid exploitation includes a provision that prohibits the assembly, possession, importation, exportation or advertising of drawings, paintings, writings, images, or films that depict persons beneath eighteen years getting on in associate in nursing indecent, obscene, or uncomplimentary manner. The draft law conjointly contains a confiscatory provision (Art. 9B).

In Australia, all States and Territories except New South Wales have publicized legislation that makes the mere possession of kid porn misbr. Legislation already existed that makes possession for the functions of distribution, sale, or exhibition against the law. In 1995, the Australian government agency initiated a national intelligence project named friend accomplishment the general public in efforts to determine the character and content of kid porn being trafficked in and out of Australia.
Europe

Legal measures designed to cope with porn vary significantly among European countries with no common approach to production, distribution, or possession of the sexy material. In European nation and Wales, the law makes it a criminal offense to require, distribute, exhibit or possess even one "indecent" photograph of a baby (Protection of youngsters Act 1978). The law defines a baby as an individual beneath sixteen. The determination of "indecency" could be a matter for the court. Within the Holland, the manufacture, dissemination, transport and export of porn involving kids beneath sixteen is prohibited (Criminal Code, Art. 240b, Sec.

1). On Apr 1995, the Code was amended to incorporate stiffer sentences and to incorporate sanctions for the mere possession of kid porn. Norway's legal code was amended in 1992. The section on child porn applies on to the introduction and possession of kid pornography however to not the assembly of such.36Section 207a of the Austrian legal code, passed in July 1994, imposes criminal sanctions for each industrial and amateur production and distribution of kid porn furthermore as for possession and/or acquisition of a similar. European nation conjointly recently created possession of kid porn associate in nursing offense beneath the German legal code. France's legal code (Penal Code Art. 227-23) forbids fixing, recording, or transmission the sexy image of a minor and therefore the distribution of that image. None of the jap European countries, with the exception of Estonia (Penal Code Art. 200/3), however, have laws specifically directed at porno.

Many European countries have terribly rigid mail secrecy laws and mails are often interfered with solely below extraordinary circumstances. To boot, European communicating authorities don't possess the police powers of U.S. communicating inspectors. Some countries have terribly strict penalties against gender with a toddler, however, flare sentences or fines for pornography. Moreover, "sting" operations that area unit routine within U.S. don't seem to be practiced in Europe.

North America the U.S. is wide thought of to be a serious client of kid creative activity however it's additionally been among the foremost aggressive in coping with perpetrators through the passage and social control of strict pornography laws. These laws (18 U.S.C. Sexually express conduct includes sexual acts yet because of the "lascivious exhibition of the genitalia or OS space of someone." A newer law (18 U.S.C. 2258) makes it a crime for someone outside U.S. territory to provide or traffic in pornography with the intent that the materials be foreign into the United States associate in nursing exterritorial application of U.S. law to lower-class .S. citizens.

Canada features a terribly comprehensive pornography law. Section 163 of the legal code makes it a criminal offense to import, produce, print, or publish any pornography which has representations of kids below eighteen World Health Organization area unit engaged in or World Health Organization area unit represented as engaged in express gender.

Furthermore, mere possession of kid creative activity is additionally currently prohibited in Canada. Regulation of laptop creative activity Since the arrival of laptop manipulated pornography, many countries have passed legislation supporting associate in nursing enlarged definition of kid creative activity which has "simulated" child porn (where the person represented is taken into account associate in nursing adult by law however is clearly depicting a child) or "pseudo" pornography which may be laptop manipulated or laptop generated pornography. Within the UK, the law expressly prohibits "pseudo-photographs" that definition includes "data keep on a laptop disc or by different electronic suggests that that is capable of conversion into a photograph". (Criminal Justice and Public Order Act 1994 Sec. 7(8)(9)). In Austria, the law prohibits not only real kid creative activity, however additionally material that suggests to Associate in Nursing objective spectator that its production concerned the sex offense of a child/minor. Similar statutes within the European country (Penal Code Sec. 240b) and in the North American nation (Penal Code Sec. 163) may well be applied to the laptop generated creative activity. Within U.S., however, the present federal kiddie porn statutes and most state statutes apply solely to depictions of actual youngsters and not "pseudo" or laptop-generated pornography. However, such "pseudo" pornography is also prosecuted consistently to federal obscenity statutes. Other countries have taken steps to control the transmission of sexually express material on the web. Recently, a Munich prosecuting attorney in FRG demanded that CompuServe block access to sexually express news teams on the web from its online service. The Gov. of Singapore has taken dramatic steps to control the web by hard-to-please that each one net server be licensed by the Gov. Singapore Broadcasting Authority. This enables them to control not solely creative activity, however, all politically sensitive material. Chinese officers have warned against the net creative activity and have recently visited Singapore to review their system of regulation.

In U.S., the Telecommunications Act of 1996, signed into law in Feb 1996, makes it a crime to wittingly transmit "obscene or indecent material" over the web or on-line laptop services if the fabric is also seen by youngsters below eighteen. directly once the linguistic communication, civil liberty and free speech teams with success sought-after a brief restraining order to dam it's social control. In Australia, 3 States have introduced bills to censor material on the web. due to the proliferation of inconsistent State and Territory laws, the commission of Attorneys General has in agreement on the preparation of a draft bill appropriate for a national theme. The passage of such legislation in several countries is disputed as a result of it directly challenges the correct freedom of expression that is very valued, significantly by the pc on-line community.

Issues associated with Privacy and Human Rights

Introduction;

Public Privacy is concerning basic flexibility and privacy rights grounded in international human rights law. Net could be a borderless public house during which nationals, paying very little relevancy their citizenship, status, ethnicity, political introduction, sexual orientation or overall foundation convey and associate.

Through new innovations, Net offers an associate setting that includes diverse members with the capability to influence and impact each other. This house is clear and two-party in its tendency but oft characterized, expanded, restricted and blue-penciled by people United Nations agency build utilization of it. Correspondence through the net is consequently frequently unknown however utilized associated imparted to an overall wide public, that stays, to the expansive part; usually obscure for the individual web shop, to be specific North American country. All things thought of, we have a tendency to do impart a number of our most non-public and individual knowledge with this unknown crowd. This overall public records nowadays around two.5 billion web users.116 within the event that Net was a nation, it'd be the largest and most inhabited nation on the world, nonetheless, with none government, body bodies, law implementation, insurance instrument, or tenets for investment, to not mention something that verges on a 'digital constitution' for all internet-nationals.

By transmission non-public info, billions of web users have effectively created virtual twins during this new house, whereas ne'er having a chance to erase info. Personal connections and 'being friends' through social networks, for instance, Renren and Facebook are often unknown in the one aspect, however, provide associate endless live of non-public info and personal messages. People's non-public and to boot skilled lives square measure publicly getting Net. Organizations and endeavors, instruction and getting ready, accounts and cash matters, non-public correspondence, and even successfulness and personaland non-public problems square measure presently by giving private info, billions of web users have formally created virtual twins during this new house, whereas ne'er having a chance to erase info. Personal connections and 'being friends' through social networks, for instance, Renren and Facebook are often unknown in the one aspect, however, provides a limitless live of non-public info and personal messages. People's non-public and additionally skilled lives square measure publicly getting Net. Organizations and undertakings, coaching and getting ready, funds and mass commercialism, non-public correspondence, and even successfulness and private problems square measure presently managed by anyone United Nations agency appearance for access thereto during this "unending" house.

The vehicle by that info moves in this house is the web and it precedes onward the interstate referred to as World Wide internet. But apparently to a national house associated domain that we have a tendency to decide a nation or a categorical, the means individuals and on-screen characters act and choose selections during this house is radio-controlled through principles and standards usually recorded in constitutions or laws.

On account of Net, these voters square measure web users all as a way and wide as potential. Albeit international governmental associations (IGOs), for instance, the UN, the Organization for the Yankee States, the African Union or the ECU Union, attempt to set international principles for the use of Net and web to be regarded and licensed by national governments, they for the foremost half neglect to do this. The purpose behind this is that states' powers and demand systems oft finish at state borders on the grounds that their order to make sure human rights are totally centered around state sovereignty and governments. IGOs and international courts frequently likewise have simply strained measures and intend to guarantee human rights, not to mention implement them. Since Net has no physical or national borders, the ways, and approaches to represent this new borderless administration aren't nonetheless characterized. In any case, within the level-headed discussion and labour to line up a Net legislation administration, human rights standards and principles, (for example, the human rights to protection, security, wellbeing, free declaration, development, and venture) provide direction to the various range of numerous performers that square measure enclosed within the definition of the Net administration and the way to conceivably management it. If at any time engineered, the Net administering body is going to be one in every of totally different stakeholders and on-screen characters together with national, international and to boot non-public playing artists, for instance, agents of organizations, social networks, NGOs, and folks.

Protection in a computer network

Privacy as a person's right is also a completely unique conception to some; but, it's truly enshrined in the United Nations Universal Declaration of Human Rights. Moreover, digital privacy is rising as a crucial right notably as a result of it might be defeated thus simply. The worldwide Network Initiative states Privacy is a human right and sponsor of human dignity'. Vital to maintaining personal security, protective identity and promoting freedom of expression within the digital age.' sadly, legislative priorities, for the most part, seem to exclude digital privacy. In line with the Electronic Frontier Foundation, the law has, however, to catch up to our evolving expectations of and wish for privacy.' See this in the U.S. wherever legislators have however to update the Electronic Communications Privacy Act of 1986. At the same time, some question the motives of presidency action (or inaction) associated categorical concern over what they understand as an overstepping of authority, notably concerning the assortment, retention, and analysis of private information. In Germany, as an example, the Supreme; the court ruled that country's information retention law unconstitutional last year.

While the long-term state of regulation concerning digital privacy is also unsure, many world firms square measure seeking to assure alignment between their human rights policies and practices and the United Nations Guiding Principles on Business and Human Rights: the

"Protect, Respect and Remedy" Framework launched formally in April 2011. Whereas the framework acknowledges the State obligation to shield human rights, it additionally acknowledges a corporate responsibility to respect human rights, act with due diligence, and address adverse impacts.' Leadership firms, like those in high technical school, are notably proactive in their efforts to handle human rights. This is often notably true of Symantec UN agency is intimately acquainted with the intersection of digital privacy and security through its core business:

"The protection of individual privacy afforded by our merchandise is vital to the protection of human rights. Indeed, several of our merchandise, as well as cryptography, terminus protection, online backup, and antivirus package support the primary 3 UNGC principles by enabling people to shield the secrecy of their communications and work merchandise, to store their info with a trustworthy merchandiser, and to watch and track makes an attempt of intrusion into their info from alternative people and/or governments."

Human Rights in Cyber house

To mention however many elementary freedoms and privacy human rights that square measure restricted during this context square measure, as an example, free expression of belief, political opinion, art and written texts; the free and equal access to information; and also the protection of privacy problems like family relations, friendships or health problems. What is more, human rights in a computer network are regarding the protection and security to be free from harassment and ill-treatment on the web for a primarily based on own political, moral or personal identity similarly for hers or his non-public skilled, educational or health information while not his or her consent? it's regarding protective own material possession and ability, i.e. art, movies, pictures, literature, scientific results, similarly as having access at any time to truthful and open trials – to call however many.

The often declared right to the internet' that aims to permit people to have access to web at any time and also the Right to be Forgotten' that assures that own non-public information remains non-public and may be deleted at any time, square measure already a part of the human rights standards regarding access to info, the correct to privacy and information protection (as within the EU elementary Rights Charta) and participation. Yet, a way to understand these rights and switch them into active legislation has got to be seen. Case law can presumably take quite your time to as certain interpretations of those rights, though the Analysis Division of the EU Court of Human Rights has already in 2011 revealed groundbreaking documents on the potential the Case-law regarding information protection and retention problems relevant for the net may mean in future choices taken by the court. During this document the liberty of expression, material possession and problems with law-breaking square measure seen the most important deficits that however have to be compelled to be additional outlined and understood through case law.

It is so now not a problem of international debates whether or not freedom rights exist or not, however, to implement and enforce them into national legislation. throughout the conference, all world organization member states confirmed that each one human right derive from the dignity and price inherent within the human person, which the human person is that the central subject of human rights and elementary freedoms, and consequently ought to be the principal beneficiary and ought to participate actively in the realization of those rights and freedoms.

Adopting cybersecurity ways that violate human rights

The use of loaded, general language has, indeed, had comprehensive consequences, as several governments area unit mistreatment imprecise internal and external threats as arguments to justify ever-larger investments in cyber arms and mass police investigation schemes, and ever larger governmental management of the net and their voters.

It has additionally given rise to the impression that every one responses area unit applicable and bonafide. As an example, as we have a tendency to found out earlier, in several countries, each democratic and nondemocratic, the threats display to national security have long been used to justify in-depth police investigation mechanisms, with a lot of and a lot of subject knowledge collected and simply accessed by state authorities. alternative ominous security' measures embrace developing alleged Internet kill switches' (the the notion of the move down the net so as to safeguard it), prescribing the utilization of secret writing, implementing filtering and obstruction mechanisms and introducing real name policies. Such measures typically create threats to civil liberties, however, they have a tendency to lack judicial oversight yet as public knowledge on that to gauge their effectiveness (often due to claims that revealing would impact on security efforts). Whereas it's not the least bit clear that they improve security, they regularly risk erasing the advantages the net brings.

Constitutional mandates

There is associate in nursing inherent and natural conflict between the rights to privacy on the one hand and also the right to info and right to understand on the opposite. A law touching on knowledge protection ought to primarily reconcile these conflicting interests.

Thus, the info of people and organizations ought to be protected in such a manner that their privacy rights don't seem to be compromised. At a similar time the proper to info U/A

19(1)(a) and also the right to understand U/A 21A law concerning knowledge protection ought to be in conformity with the subsequent mandates, as obligatory by the sacred and inviolable Constitution of India:

Right to privacy U/A 21: The law of privacy is that the recognition of the individuals right to be including and to own his personal house inviolate. The term —privacy‖ denotes the rightful claim of the individual to see the extent to that he desires to share of himself with others and his management over the time, place and circumstances to speak with others. It suggests that his right to withdraw or to participate as he thinks match. It additionally suggests that the individuals right to regulate the dissemination of knowledge concerning him because it is his own personal possession. Privacy primarily considerations the individual. It, therefore, relates to and overlaps with the construct of liberty. The foremost serious advocates of privacy should confess that there unit serious issues of the process the essence and scope of the proper. Privacy interest in autonomy should even be placed within the context of alternative rights and values. The proper to privacy as Associate in nursing freelance and distinctive construct originated within the field of wrongful conduct law, beneath that a replacement explanation for action for damages ensuing from unlawful invasion of privacy was recognized. This right has 2 aspects that area unit however 2 faces of a similar coin: (1) the overall law of privacy that affords a wrongful conduct action for damages ensuing from Associate in nursing unlawful invasion of privacy, and (2) the constitutional recognition given to the proper to privacy that protects personal privacy against unlawful governmental invasion. The primary facet of this right should be same to own been desecrated wherever, as an example, a person name or likeness is employed, while not his consent for advertising or not- advertising functions or for that matter, his life is written whether or not praising or otherwise and printed while not his consent. In recent times, however, this right has non-heritable a constitutional standing. India may be a human to the International Covenant on Civil and Political Rights, 1966. Article17 thence provides for the —right of privacy‖. Article12 of the Universal Declaration of Human Rights, 1948 is almost in similar terms. Article seventeen of the International Covenant doesn't go contrary to any a part of our municipal law. Article21 of the Constitution has, therefore, to be taken in conformity with the jurisprudence.

Data Technology and therefore the Law of Privacy

Advances in engineering and telecommunications have dramatically increased the quantity of data that may be kept, retrieved, accessed and collected almost instantly. Within the net age, data is therefore centralized and then simply accessible that one faucet on a button may present surprising amounts of data regarding a private. In terms of electronic data, someone ought to be in a position to keep personal affairs to himself. Advances in engineering area unit creating it simple to try to do what was not possible shortly pass. Data in several databases are cross-matched to make profiles of people and to even predict their behavior. This behavior is determined by individual transactions with numerous instructional, financial, governmental, skilled and judicial establishments. Major uses of this data embody marketing and credit check services for potential borrowers or renters. To the individual, the result of all this data sharing is most typically seen as increased —junk mail‖.

There unit rather more serious privacy problems to be thought about. For instance:

i. whenever you log onto the web you allow behind Associate in Nursing electronic trail. Websites and advertising firms area unit able to track users as they travel on the web to assess their personal preferences, habits, and lifestyles. This data is employed for marketing campaigns that concentrate on the individual client. Whenever you utilize your MasterCard, you allow behind a path of wherever you shopped and once, what you got, your whole preferences, your favorite edifice.

ii. Employees privacy is underneath military blockade as employers habitually use computer code to access their employees e-mail and each move of the worker. Field sales representatives have their movements half-tracked by the employment of location-based pursuit systems in new wireless phones. Thus, the law of privacy has not unbroken pace with the technological development. It should be noted that the correct freedom of speech and expression and right to privacy area unit 2 sides of the same coin. One persons right to understand and be informed could violate another right to be let alone. These rights should be harmoniously construed in order that they're properly promoted with the minimum of such understood and necessary restrictions. The law of privacy endeavors to balance this competitive freedom.

Freedom of data knowledge U/A 19(1) (a): the correct to impart and receive information is a species of the correct freedom of speech and expression. A subject incorporates an elementary Right to use the most effective suggests that of conveyance and receiving data. The State isn't solely underneath Associate in nursing obligation to respect the elemental Rights of the voters, however conjointly equally underneath Associate in nursing obligation to confirm conditions underneath that the correct meaningfully and effectively

164

be enjoyed by one and every one. Freedom of speech and expression is basic to and indivisible by from a democratic polity. The globe has stirred towards universalization of right to freedom of expression. During this context, reference is also created to Article ten of the EU Convention on Human Rights. Article ten of the Convention provides that everybody incorporates a right to freedom of expression and this right shall embody freedom to carry opinions and to receive data and concepts while not interference by the general public authorities and in spite of the frontiers.

Again, Article 19(1) and 19(2) of the International Covenant on Civil and Political Rights declares that everybody shall have the correct to carry opinions while not interference and everybody shall have the correct freedom of expression, and this right shall embody freedom to hunt, receive and impart data of concepts of every kind in spite of frontiers, either orally, in writing or in print, within the variety of art or through the other media of his selection. Within the Indian context, Article 19(1) (a) of the constitution guarantees to all or any citizens‖ freedom of speech and expression. At the same time, Article 19(2) permits the State to create any law in up to now intrinsically law imposes cheap restrictions on the exercise of the rights given by Article 19(1) (a) of the constitution within the interest of sovereignty and integrity of Republic of India, the safety of the State, friendly relations with foreign States, public order, decency, morality, contempt of court, defamation and incitement of offense. Thus, a subject incorporates a right to receive data which right comes from the conception of freedom of speech and expression comprised in Article 19(1) (a). It must, however, be noted that freedoms underneath Article nineteen, including

Article 19(1) (a), are accessible solely to voters of India. Associate in nursing alien or foreigner has no rights beneath this text as a result of he's not a national of India. Therefore to confer protection upon non-citizens one needs to rely upon and apply Article twenty one that is obtainable to any or all persons, whether or not national or non-citizen.

Right to know to beneath stand to grasp under Article twenty-one: Article 21 enshrines right to life and private liberty. The expressions right to life and private liberty' are concise terms, which embrace inside themselves sort of rights and attributes. A number of them also are found in Article nineteen and therefore have 2 sources at a similar time.

In R.P. restricted v Indian specific Newspapers the Supreme Court scan into Article 21 the proper to understand. The Supreme Court command that right to understand could be a necessary ingredient of democratic democracy. Seeable of international developments once distances are shrinking, international communities are coming back along for cooperation in varied spheres and that they are moving towards international perspective in various fields as well as Human Rights, the expression liberty' should receive associate in nursing expanded that means. The expression cannot be restricted to the mere absence of bodily restraint. It's wide enough to expand to full vary of rights as well as right to carry a specific opinion and right to sustain and nurture that opinion. For sustaining and nurturing that opinion it becomes necessary to receive info. Article twenty one confers on all persons a right to understand that embrace a right to receive info. The reach and scope of Article twenty-one are far wider as compared to Article 19(1) (a). Thus, the courts are needed to expand its scope by the approach of rendering. In P.U.C.L v U.O.I the Supreme Court determined that elementary Rights themselves don't have any mounted contents, most of them are empty vessels into that every generation should pour its contents within the light-weight of its expertise. The try of the court ought to be to expand the reach and reach of the basic Rights by the method of judicial interpretation. There can not be any distinction between the basic Rights mentioned in Chapter-III of the constitution and therefore the declaration of such rights on the basis of the judgments‖ rendered by the Supreme Court. Further, it is well settled that whereas decoding the constitutional provisions managing elementary Rights the courts should not forget the principles embodied within the international conventions and instruments and as way as potential the courts should offer impact to the principles contained in those instruments. The courts beneath associate in nursing obligation to grant due respect to the international conventions and norms whereas construing the domestic laws, additional thus once there's no inconsistency or conflict between them and therefore the domestic law.

Statutory perspective

The inherent and natural conflict between the right to understand and right to privacy is additionally per meative varied statutory laws enacted from time to time. These laws, with their conflicting contours, are:

Right to info in cases of genital or infectious diseases: The welfare of the society is that the primary duty of each civilized State. Sections 269 to 271 of the Indian Penal Code, 1860 create Associate in the nursing act, that is possible to unfold infection, punishable by considering it as associate in the nursing offense. These sections are framed so as to forestall folks from doing acts, that possible to unfold infectious diseases. therefore a person tormented by associate in nursing infectious malady is beneath associate in nursing obligation to disclose a similar to the opposite person and if he fails to try and do thus he are at risk of being prosecuted beneath these sections. As a corollary, the opposite person includes a right to understand regarding such communicable disease. In Mr. X v Hospital Z the Supreme Court command that it absolutely was receptive, the hospital authorities or the doctor involved to reveal such info to the persons associated with the woman whom he meant to marry and she or he had a right to understand regarding the HIV Positive standing of the appellant. an issue might, however, be raised that if the person tormented by HIV Positive marries with a willing partner once revealing the factum of malady thereto partner, can he still commit Associate in Nursing offense inside the that means of Section 269 and 270 of I.P.C. it's submitted that there ought to be no bar for such a wedding if the healthy domestic partner consents to marry despite being tuned in to the very fact that the opposite domestic partner is tormented by the aforementioned malady.

The courts shouldn't interfere with the selection of 2 willing adults-United Nations agency are willing to marry one another with full data regarding the malady. It should be noted that in a mister. X v Hospital Z (II) a 3 decide bench of the Supreme Court command that after the division bench of the Supreme Court command that the revelation of HIV Positive standing was even because the woman includes a right to understand, there was no want for this court to travel any and declare generally on what rights and obligations arise

in such context on right to privacy or whether or not such persons are entitled to marry or not or within the event such persons marry they'd commit associate in nursing offense beneath the law or whether or not such right is suspended throughout the amount of ill health. Therefore, all those observations created by the court within the aforementioned matter were spare. Thus, the court command that the observations created by this court, except to the extent of holding that the appellants right wasn't affected in any manner by revealing his HIV Positive standing to the relatives of his fiancée, are uncalled for. It looks that the court has complete the untenably of the sooner observations and therefore the sensible difficulties, which can arise once the revelation of HIV standing.

Misuse of privacy and human rights

The Information Technology Act, 2000 provides for 2 measures, just in case of wrongful revealing and misuse of private information, i.e. a civil consequence of payment of compensation and criminal consequence of social control for the commission of the offense. below Section 43A of the IT Act, 2000, a body company World Health Organization is possessing, dealing or handling any sensitive personal information or data, and is negligent in implementing and maintaining cheap security practices leading to wrongful loss or wrongful gain to a person, then such a body company could also be control vulnerable to pay damages to the person thus affected.

Online Disputes Resolutions (ODR)

Introduction;

It primarily involves negotiation, mediation or arbitration, or a mixture of all 3. During this respect it's typically seen as being the net equivalent of other dispute resolution (ADR). To court disputes and interstate conflicts. its believed that economic mechanisms to resolve online disputes can impact within the development of e-commerce. whereas the appliance of ODR isn't restricted to disputes arising out of business to shopper(B2C) online transactions, it appears to be notably apt for these disputes, since it's logical to use an equivalent medium (the internet) for the resolution of e-commerce disputes once parties square measure of times situated off from each other.

ODR may be an extremely suggested methodology as a result of it's not as time intensive as traditional legal proceeding, disputes square measure simply documented and therefore the person needn't withstand the jurisdiction of any court. There square measure 3 main models of online dispute settlement:

1. **Cyber Settle:** Whereby there's machine-driven negotiation mechanism.

2. **On-line mediation:** Whereby there's live mediation.

3. **On-line adjudication:** Whereby there's online arbitration According to her, the Arbitration and Conciliation Act, 1996, and therefore the data Act, 2000, square measure well equipped to cater to the new system of dispute resolution. The steps that require to be taken are:

1. Produce additional awareness.

2. Draft rules just in case of any ambiguity.

3. Extend the system by promoting it all told legislations.

4. Parties ought to be created to sign a binding agreement before they enter into the net dispute resolution system.

Online dispute resolution is straightforward, speedy and provides a simple and prompt means of partitioning issues for parties that square measure in several components of the planet.

Delhi supreme court has e-courts however they're not as purposeful as they got to be. However, once they're used properly, it'll be done to own a palmy arbitration system. The Supreme Court has already set up on this issue and held that selecting Associate in nursing umpire on-line is valid. Consistent with Justice fractional monetary unit., paper filing etc. ought to have already been done away with since e- filing is that the order of the day.

Evolution of ODR business

Online dispute resolution (ODR) was developed to bypass clogged and slow-moving courts and therefore the trouble of physical dispute resolution mechanisms. ODR tries to harness the ability of net to resolve disputes, by reducing prices, doing away with the need to trip attend courts and usually creating the whole method quicker and economical through use of internet-based mostly technologies. This can be the essential precept on that ODR is constructed. If doable, this might be a big improvement over the present different dispute resolution ways like ancient arbitration, mediation etc. ODR debuted in 1998 in U.S. and not a lot of is understood regarding it in the Asian country.

Partitioning Business Dispute

For business, time is cash. Disputes square measure like cancer that ought to be stopped from spreading as before long as doable. The business disputes could also be business to business (B2B) or business to the client(B2C). For each form of disputes, litigation is the least favored methodology of resolution for a spread of reasons – delay being the foremost. ADR ways give the answer. Ways like negotiation, mediation, conciliation, arbitration and a mixture of those are used and square measure presently changing into in style for resolution of business disputes. However, the limitation of those ways, notably, the physical presence of each the parties and therefore the arbitrator/conciliator/mediator at one place a variety of conferences, makes even ADR ways quite cumbersome and ineffective.

There square measure 3 current approaches to ODR: Net, non-adjudicative ADR, and arbitration. The primary centers on the web and knowledge technology. The principle underlying the Net approach is to search out higher, quicker and cheaper ways in which to resolve disputes with the help of technology. The non-adjudicative ADR approach to ODR focuses principally on negotiation and mediation, and however to enhance each communication and relationships between parties. The arbitration approach emphasizes rights associate in nursing applications of law to resolve the dispute with an arbitrators call. The impetus behind this approach is that the success of ancient arbitration. If it works thus well offline, then it ought to be custom-made on-line, the reasoning goes.

The major players in ODR are a profession, consumers, and government and ADR establishments. Profession favors ODR as a result of it's personal, quick and cheap. It additionally encourages client trust. For client organizations, ODR enforces client rights. Governments see ODR as a tool to supply access to justice that courts don't seem to be nonetheless equipped to supply, decrease court congestion and more the e-commerce economy. ADR establishments see ODR as a chance to realize the competitive edge. The applying of data communication technology (ICT) is evolving as a vital means that for future resolution of sure sorts of conflict. ODR can become associate in the nursing progressively necessary element of the infrastructure needed if online business and different relationships square measure to appreciate their full potential.

Globally, the employment of ODR is growing and has been well documented over the years and client disputes square measure seen because of the main space of growth, along with human resources, government and employment disputes additionally a fertile ground for this sort of technology.

Why ODR?

Cost and Time;

ODR is mostly thought of an additional economical method than ADR/ legal proceeding as a result of its faster and fewer expensive. Given the very fact, it doesn't need a physical presence as is that the case with ADR and legal proceeding, it saves au courant time and price as could also be needed.

Modus Operandi. The mode of proceedings in ODR is usually determined by the parties in contrast to court based mostly suits that follow a strict statute determined procedure. Of course, ODR should follow the foundation ordered down by acceptable legislation and a few basic principles that each one legal proceeding ought to follow, however, it's the potential to emerge as an additional versatile and convenient mode of dispute resolution. Also, ODR is usually less resistance as a result of it takes place in a very abundant less formal setting on an internet platform.

Confidentiality of matter is protected much better in associate in nursing ODR method.

Flexibility ODR is way additional versatile because it is ruled by party agreement or the foundations and regulations of the net platform used and aren't obsessed with the stare (deciding on the premise of precedents) principle rather like the other ADR.

Online and Offline Model of ODR

The potential use of the web to resolve international disputes is divided into 2 distinct areas: exploitation Internet-related technology to resolve real world's disputes online or part on-line and exploitation the web to resolve disputes arising on the web itself. For instance, in offline dispute, you'll be able to have a clause in your contract together with your provider for resolution of dispute exploitation one among the ODR platforms. As so much as on-line disputes square measure involved, the platform you're addressing may need Associate in the Nursing inherent mechanism as is that the case with eBay.

Procedures adopted for ODR;

Online Negotiation

Forums such as Cyber Settle use negotiation for Dispute Resolution. On-line negotiation is of 2 sorts, closed model and open model.

Close Model-

The common characteristic of those processes is that the parties‖ submission of financial offers and demands that don't seem to be disclosed to their negotiating counterpart, however square measure compared by pc in rounds. If the supply and demand match, fall at intervals an outlined vary or overlap the case is settled for the type of the supply and demand, the matching quantity, or the demand within the event of associate in the nursing overlap. If the claim is settled, the participant square measure in real time notified via email.

Open Model-

Under the open model, a celebration will read the others party supply or demand solely after having created a requirement or supply.

Whenever any supply is at intervals twenty percent of any demand, there's settlement of the median.

Online Mediation-

A typical on-line mediation procedure takes place as follows. The litigator initiates it by finishing a confidential kind on the provider website. Then, a mediator contacts the respondent so as for him/her to participate. Each party set forth the mediation ground rules.

The intermediator communicates with the parties, typically collectively and typically separately, to facilitate Associate in nursing agreement. If associate in the nursing agreement is reached, it always takes the shape of writing.

Thus, the net method doesn't take issue a great deal from the offline method, aside from the swollen use of technology. Email is that the mediators succor for functions of framing and moving the discussion forward. However, email was already used by offline mediators. In on-line mediation, websites like good Settle, Legal bully off etc. square measure providing on-line mediators with new tools to supplement email with different communication tools together with electronic conferencing, online chat, video-conferencing, facsimile, and phone.

Online arbitration

Online arbitration income on totally different communication stages (process agreement, initial displays, rebuttals, thought, and decision). Arbitration is generally a far simpler communication method than mediation. Within the simplest arbitration, code that enables positions to be explicit and documents to be shared could offer a decent frame for the method.

175

There area unit several arbitration service suppliers in abroad such as Yankee Arbitration Association. An aortic aneurysm is understood for handling massive, advanced cases. In 2011, forty-sixth of the arbitration filed with an aortic aneurysm concerned claims $1,000,000 or more.

ODR vs Proceedings

In ODR, price and time potency area unit typical characteristics as against a judicial method with consumes substantial time and value for assessment of disputes. Tyler and Bretherton with competence stated- A the problem of utilizing ancient dispute resolution strategies in low worth cross-border disputes has a light-emitting diode to interest in low price cases, cross territorial dispute resolution methods'. ODR denotes bigger flexibility because it may be initiated at any purpose of a legal proceeding or even before a judicial proceeding begins. ODR will conjointly be terminated if the parties reciprocally decide that it isn't resulting in a practical answer. The parties have the autonomy to choose the mode and procedure for online dispute resolution just in case disputes arise from a selected e-contract. Even within the absence of a written contract declaring ODR as the methodology of dispute resolution, the parties could adopt ODR strategies to resolve their disputes once such disputes arise. Contrary to proceedings, the parties area unit liberated to select their governing law of contract, the procedure to resolve disputes, elect associate in nursing ODR service supplier and supply for alternative incidental matters. Use of ODR conjointly permits the choice of neutral third party from associate in nursing knowledgeable about a panel of mediator/arbitrators which implies bigger inclination and parties could gift their case on their own while not apprehension that their son-public disputes can flow into the general public domain through judicial precedents. The disputes and also the negotiations that turn out between parties remain confidential in the least times.

Benefits

Economically viable: price is one among the foremost crucial factors under consideration resolution, as disputants wish to reach associate in nursing optimum call at very cheap doable worth. ODR most accurately fits the money demands of all parties to a dispute, as most of the document area unit changed via e-mail and also the proceedings come about online as against exchange of documents by post. The costs associated with travel and accommodation, the venue for conducting the proceedings is additionally eliminated. Therefore, finishing up ODR isn't solely easier and quicker, however, it's conjointly considerably cheaper Speedy resolution: one among the most blessings of ODR over typical ADR is that it's less-time intense. Where in ADR it should take many months to resolve a dispute, ODR guarantees settlement of disputes inside some weeks. Further, the borderless nature of the net diminishes the communication issues round-faced by parties and their counsels WHO are also settled in numerous time zones. Moreover, the net allows parties to simply get information and alternative data concerning their cases in real time. Additionally, to straightforward accessibility, email simplifies the task of programming ODR proceedings and avoids any phone or fax- tags within the method. The net is additionally a superior and swifter type of communication because it facilitates the causation and storing of documents of multiple parties at the same time, so saving each time and cash.

Non-confrontational mechanism: By removing the physical presence of the resister, ODR allows the adjudicating body to dispassionately resolve the dispute, strictly on basis of the reserves of the case. Further, since most of the arguments or dialogues come about asynchronously over the net, it permits the disputants to replicate on their positions before articulating their response. In addition, such a mechanism neutralizes any economic or alternative power disparities that could get between the disputants, as there could be many instances wherever one party to the dispute may be an unimportant manufacturer/supplier and also the opposite party is world entity. Neutral forum: the net offers a neutral forum for assessment and also advantage' one among the parties so far enjoyed.

Facilitates record keeping: ODR facilitates the method of maintaining the record of the correspondences, pleadings, statements, and alternative written, oral or visual communications, by relying entirely on digital records. This, in turn, saves time and cash of the parties.

ODR in India

2000 in India, e-commerce, and e-governance are given a proper and legal recognition in India. Even the normal arbitration law of India has been reformulated and currently, India has Arbitration and Conciliation Act, 1996 in situ that's satisfying the harmonical standards of UNCITRAL Model.

ODR in India is facing several legal roadblocks and therefore the same got to be addressed in real time by the Indian government. Further, awareness regarding ODR in India is additionally missing as per ODR service suppliers in India.

ODR in Asia

Asia could be a made and major continent that has excelled within the utilization of ICTs. While the several Asian States benefit a mention, this chapter shall specialize in China, Japan, and India as major ODR players within the Asian continent. The choice of such 3 states isn't solely because of their international standing and weight, however additionally because of the progressive and accelerated development within the invention and implementation of ICT applications, that actually impacts the event of ODR schemes. On such account, the chapter shall be divided into 3 halves; every part shall be dedicated to assessing the establishment of ODR in one in all the 3 distinguished states, that have 3 of the best web and movable stage rates within the world.

For example, China has emerged collectively of the biggest e-commerce giants with quite 457 million web users and 277 million movable web users. In Japan, a written report entitled Basic IT Strategy', discharged in August 2000 by the Ministry of International Trade and business (MITI), has disclosed Japans ambition to expand its IT infrastructure in support of not solely the event of e-commerce, however the ultimate implementation of e-Government initiatives.

Drawbacks

The following drawbacks prevail within the ODR method that hampers its growth as an associate degree economical mechanism for partitioning disputes:

Lack of human interaction and miscommunication: The lack of face-to-face interaction deprives the adjudicating authority of the chance to gauge the believability of parties and therefore the witnesses. Moreover, the impersonal nature of the net will probably cause miscommunication between the parties, that is probably going to occur once parties area unit placed totally different in several in numerous countries and speak different languages.

Limited vary of disputes: Like ADR, ODR is additionally best suited to resolve solely sure styles of disputes, like, e-commerce and name disputes. The ODR mechanism might not be appropriate for partitioning all kinds of online dispute, for instance, negotiation and mediation could also be a lot of appropriate in partitioning problems like the damages that will be due for breach of contract.

Inadequate confidentiality and secrecy of proceedings: The secrecy of proceedings is key to the method of dispute resolution, that ODRs inherits from ADRs. Consequently, ODR suppliers have created technological arrangements, such as installation of varied softwares, firewalls, etc., to protect the information sent by the parties from information interception, alteration, etc. Though substantial efforts are created towards creation and implementation of knowledge protection laws, these measures don't guarantee 100 percent protection from hackers and alternative cyber offenders and need constant change, despite that there should exist loop-holes which may be exploited. Thus, inadequate web security could act as a significant deterrent to the growth of ODR Inadequate authenticity: Closely associated with the problem of security is that the issue of authentic identification of the user. In associate degree ADR method, one party will be sure that the opposite party it's addressing is that the party really concerned about the dispute. However, in a computer network.

Simpletoughroughchallenginghardharshdangerousdifficultdemanding tasking to verify the credibleness of messages received and it's comparatively easy for a 3rd party to impersonate or misrepresent one in all the parties within the dispute, inflicting confusion, thereby defeating the terrible.

Purpose of adopting ODR

Jurisdiction: web being a borderless medium transcends and challenges traditional ideas of jurisdiction. This leads to the downside in deciding the applicable substantive law that is to be applied to the dispute. This issue will solely be resolved by parties clearly distinguishing the applicable substantive and procedural laws within the clause whereby they conform to submit the dispute to resolution by ODR. Ultimately, the resolution of this issue would be contingent upon the declaration of the court systems in numerous jurisdiction which might examine and interpret such ODR clauses, however, this method is ineluctable and inevitable and can't be circumvented.

Hindrances at the pre-trial stage: a big element of the pre-trial stage is discovery; interrogatories and collation of proof to support the various contentions of the parties. This discovery or investigatory method could be decreased within the ODR method to hurry the method of settlement of the dispute. However, in a very scenario wherever the facts area unit controversial, a restricted discovery procedure could serve to limit the truth-finding capability of the adjudicating authority to get the true and correct statement of facts. Further, limiting or eliminating discovery method could offend the group action, inflicting the courts to strike them down as they are doing not meet the minimum necessities of group action.

Publication of proceedings and award: If ODR is to be inspired as a well-liked mode of dispute resolution, details of proceedings and selections would be needed to be revealed that ensures transparency. But, this contradicts the terrible essence of ODR, that is respecting the confidentiality and right to privacy of the parties. Thus, the fate of ODR hangs in balance with one faculty of thought exacting absolute secrecy of proceedings and therefore the alternative faculty seeking publication of proceedings and therefore the selections. As a matter of following, currently, all ODR suppliers keep the proceedings confidential and unleashing providing each the parties conform to publish the choice.

Difficulty in social control of online awards: Like ADRs, within the case of on-line arbitrations, once the choice has been rendered, a similar needs to be enforced within the acceptable court. In many jurisdictions, together with India, the orders in execution area unit subject to appeals and this serves to extend the method of execution. Going by this principle, unless the parties area unit assured of the social control and implementation of the choices, disputants might not have abundant religion in on-line proceedings. Further, enforceability of foreign selections pronounced once completion of ODR proceedings is additionally a problem that should be thought of whereas agreeing to associate degree ODR clause.

Challenging associate degree award: Since ODR proceedings area unit conducted online, another issue requiring clarity is that the intervention of a court throughout or once the completion of the proceedings and/or declaration of the choice. This may once more raise the question of (a) the social control of call the choice of the court within the country wherever the alternative party operates/resides; and (b) appeals against the choice of the court and social control of the aforesaid decision.

Way forward for ODR

As aforesaid by Jeffrey N. Rosenthal is an associate degree professional person with Blank Rome, the attractiveness of ODR services to the world-at-large can probably solely increase. The supply of such systems will build trust in a very company by reminding shoppers and companies addressing it that a neutral third-party will cheaply and simply resolve disputes.

However, India is nonetheless to exploit the advantages of ODR. There is associate degree acute lack of legislative action or awareness in this regard. This downside is teamed up with the shortage of ODR establishments in India. Given the actual fact that it is being expected that the SME Sector would be the propulsion for growth in India, there's immense scope for application of ODR Mechanism in resolution of dispute for SMEs as ODR will be an inexpensive and simple answer of a disputes that area unit guaranteed to arise throughout the course of business.

Electronic commerce brings each comfort and discomforts to its users. The comforts embrace the spot sales and get, competitive prices, convenience, Saving of your time, etc. The discomforts embrace frauds and cyber crimes committed against e-commerce users. Sometimes there area unit disagreements and dissatisfactions in addition among patrons and purchasers that can't be resolved victimization ancient proceedings strategies. This is the rationale why we'd like various dispute resolution (ADR) mechanism to resolve e-commerce disputes in India. E-commerce laws and laws in India area unit restricted in nature and this doesn't enable the use of ADR mechanisms and technology-driven solutions. For example, whereas EC and alternative nations area unit progressively victimization online dispute resolution (ODR) for partitioning several aspects of e-commerce disputes nonetheless online dispute resolution (ODR) in India remains not acknowledged.

Similarly, the institution of e-courts in of India may also facilitate early and effective e-commerce disputes resolutions in India. However, until October 2012 we have a tendency to area unit still anticipating the institution of 1st e-court in India. E-courts and ODR in India area unit desperately needed to cut back backlog of cases and for reducing increasing pressure upon ancient courts. E-courts and ODR may also facilitate in e-commerce disputes resolutions in India.

Misuse of ODR

When records area unit promiscuously accessible, there's a risk of invasion of privacy or misuse of knowledge. Technology should still adapt to associate degree setting within which challenges to privacy and therefore the security of knowledge area unit commonplace. The resolution of disputes on-line could gift new challenges to the protection of steer. One in all the largest technological obstacles to beat is that the lack of private association inherent in conducting a court or ODR continuing electronically.

www.ingramcontent.com/pod-product-compliance
Lightning Source LLC
Chambersburg PA
CBHW071247050326
40690CB00011B/2292